# CRAFT CAPITAL

## Philadelphia's Cultures of Making

# CRAFT CAPITAL

Philadelphia's
Cultures
of Making

# CAPITAL

# CRAFT CAPITAL

### Philadelphia's Cultures of Making

Edited by Glenn Adamson

With contributions by

Elisabeth Agro

Sarah Archer

Chad Curtis

Anthony Elms

Elizabeth Essner

Michelle Millar Fisher

Jessica Kourkounis

Don Miller

Jennifer-Navva Milliken

Heather Gibson Moqtaderi

Kelli Morgan

Jennifer Zwilling

Photography by Jessica Kourkounis

  SCHIFFER PUBLISHING

4880 Lower Valley Road · Atglen, PA 19310

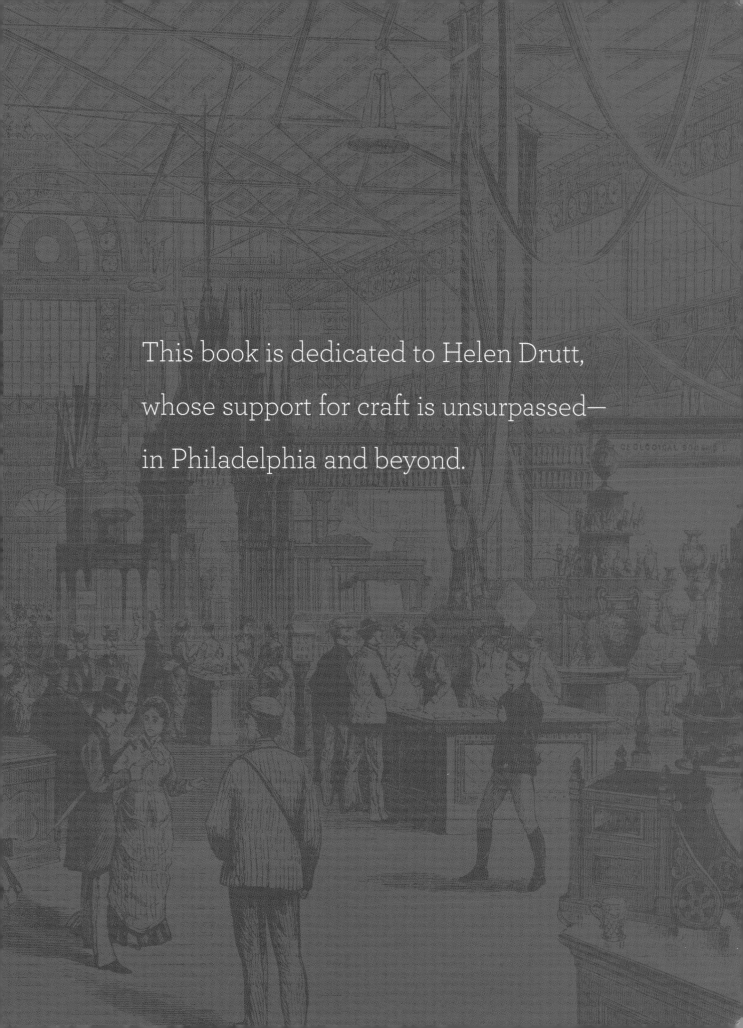

This book is dedicated to Helen Drutt,
whose support for craft is unsurpassed—
in Philadelphia and beyond.

# TABLE *of* CONTENTS

*Photo Essays by Jessica Kourkounis*

## FOREWORD

CraftNOW Philadelphia is proud to have produced *Craft Capital: Philadelphia's Cultures of Making*, in commemoration of our fifth anniversary as a collaborative showcasing our city as a national center of craft and making.

The concept for CraftNOW emerged from a chance meeting of Clara Hollander and David Seltzer following their visits to Art Basel Miami several years ago. Each noted how inspiring it was to see the role that an art-and-design festival could play in transforming a city both culturally and economically. They resolved to explore whether a smaller, nonprofit "craft-centric" version could be launched locally, building on Philadelphia's long-standing history as a craft center and the continuing popularity of the Philadelphia Museum of Art (PMA) Contemporary Craft Show, held each November.

The initial meeting in 2014 brought together leaders from Philadelphia's nonprofit craft sector: Sean Buffington, then president of the University of the Arts; Thora Jacobson, then executive director of the Philadelphia Art Alliance; Albert LeCoff, cofounder of the Center for Art in Wood; Chris Taylor, then director of the Clay Studio; and Nancy O'Meara, show manager for the PMA Craft Show. They received great encouragement from three Philadelphia-based thought leaders in the Craft movement: Helen Drutt and Ruth and Rick Snyderman.

Joined by many other institutions, galleries, and individuals, the consortium identified the following objectives for CraftNOW:

- Unite, support, and promote the region's craft organizations through coordinated, thematic exhibitions, symposiums, events, marketing, and branding;

- Engage, educate, and expose students of all ages to all craft disciplines; and

- Promote the vitality of Philadelphia's cultural scene and generate economic growth.

CraftNOW launched our first series of events in the Fall of 2015, with Maria Moller serving as acting program manager. Since then, CraftNOW has grown steadily in breadth and depth under the able direction of Leila Cartier, a curator, artist, and our executive director, assisted by our Board of Overseers. The University of the Arts, under President and CEO David Yager, has been incredibly supportive in serving as CraftNOW's fiscal agent and hosting events.

The CraftNOW consortium today consists of nearly three dozen organizations throughout the Delaware River valley: materials-based centers such as the Clay Studio, the Center for Art in Wood, and the Fabric Workshop and Museum; higher-educational institutions such as the University of the Arts, Moore College of Art & Design, Tyler School of Art at Temple University, and Pennsylvania Academy of the Fine Arts: regional institutions such as Wayne Arts Center and the Wharton Esherick Museum; the PMA Craft Show, through the Women's Committee of the Philadelphia Museum of Art (PMA); and many more public and private organizations.

We now have firmly taken root in Philadelphia's cultural landscape, sponsoring such signature events as citywide multivenue exhibitions around a common theme; CraftNOW Create, a hands-on demonstrations of craft held each November in the lobby of the Kimmel Center for the Performing Arts, attracting hundreds of visitors; and our annual symposium, with nationally renowned keynote speakers Glenn Adamson, Abraham Thomas, and Robert

Lugo. We also promote craft-related activities around the region through social media and on our website (craftnowphila.org). The city, through mayoral proclamation, now designates November as "CraftMONTH," recognizing the importance of craft and making in the city.

We are grateful to the contributors (as of this writing), including the Center for American Art of the Philadelphia Museum of Art and Poor Richard's Charitable Trust, whose significant funding helped initiate this project. A major gift from the Virginia and Harvey Kimmel Arts Education Fund of the Philadelphia Foundation was leveraged as a challenge grant answered by the following individuals and institutions:

Barbara Adams

Wendy and Mort Branzburg

Jane Davis

Ddora Foundation

Dovetail Wood Arts, LLC

Sherry and Brian Effron

Patricia and Gordon Fowler

Gravers Lane Gallery and Goldenberg Group

Bruce Kardon

Danielle Rice

Karyn Scher

The Women's Committee of the Philadelphia Museum of Art

Zeldin Family Foundation

Additional gifts were received from Rosemarie Fabien and Tom Normile, Richard R. Goldberg, Merryll Saylan, Judith Schaechter, and Susan Thompson and Don Miller.

Philadelphia has been a leading center for craft for well over 250 years, and the tradition continues today. The city is home to a wide variety of organizations dedicated to the field: strong galleries, world-class museums, and thriving higher-education programs. All of this makes a perfect creative ecosystem. On behalf of CraftNOW's Board of Overseers, we hope you enjoy this book, which serves both as an introduction and an invitation to Philadelphia's dynamic world of making.

Clara Hollander and David Seltzer, cofounders

CraftNOW Board of Overseers
Clara Hollander, president
Elissa Topol, vice president
Christina Copeland, treasurer
David Seltzer, secretary

Josephine Burri
Patricia Fowler
Bill Gehrman
Albert LeCoff
Jacqueline Lewis
Brenton McCloskey
Jennifer-Navva Milliken
Julie Siglin
Thadeus Suzenski
Emily Zilber
Jennifer Zwilling
Leila Cartier, executive director

*by*

*Glenn Adamson*

# In 1751, having been rung only once, the Liberty Bell was smashed apart with a sledgehammer. It wasn't called the Liberty Bell then, of course. It acquired that name only when it was embraced as a symbol by the antislavery abolitionist movement a full century later. But already it had cracked, on the very first attempt to make it sound. One can imagine how dismaying this was, all the more so given that it had been shipped all the way over from London.

OPPOSITE | THE PROCESS OF MAKING BELLS AT MALMARK

Two local brass founders, John Stow and John Pass, were assigned to remake it. They broke the great bell into pieces, melted it down, and then remade it using the original metal, with the addition of many pounds of copper to improve the alloy. They almost certainly had no experience casting such a large object. Yet, after one false start (which made a sound "like two coal scuttles banged together") and another recasting, they managed it. The bell was hung in the tower of the State House—today's Independence Hall—seeing many decades of use until it once again failed. The current famous crack, suspiciously neat, was actually hand-drilled—a failed repair, dating to 1846. And so the bell passed out of use, and into the realm of symbol.[1]

Today, the Liberty Bell is an emblem not only of Philadelphia, but also of American freedom, surpassed in fame only by the Statue of Liberty (the work of French artisans, rather than British ones). Even if it did not have that status, however, it would be unbeatable as an icon of Philadelphia craft. Combined in the story of the Liberty Bell are the city's most enduring qualities: a concentration of skilled makers, adaptive in the face of adversity; connections to other, larger urban centers; and an ever-evolving relationship to its own history.

This book explores these themes through a series of contributions by writers and curators based in and around the city. Sarah Archer's introductory essay explains how Philadelphia first asserted itself as a national craft capital and has continually reconnected with that heritage, particularly following the Second World War. That period saw numerous artists establish their practices in Philadelphia. Just as important, a network of museums, schools, galleries (like those of Helen Drutt, Rick and Ruth Snyderman, and Jane Korman), and nonprofit organizations (including the Clay Studio, Center for Art in Wood, and Fabric Workshop) emerged to support them. The other authors in the volume

Today, the Liberty Bell is an emblem not only of Philadelphia, but also of American freedom, surpassed in fame only by the Statue of Liberty (the work of French artisans, rather than British ones). Even if it did not have that status, however, it would be unbeatable as an icon of Philadelphia craft.

concentrate on different aspects of the contemporary making scene in Philadelphia, which is extraordinarily diverse and active, taking its energies from technological experimentation, community activism, contemporary art, and the resonant past.

The book is also enlivened by a specially commissioned series of photographs by Jessica Kourkounis, which together constitute a visual essay on the many textures of Philadelphia craft. Among the images she has captured is another iconic Philadelphia phenomenon, the Mummers Parade. Performed annually on New Year's Day, this folk spectacle has been a creative outlet for the city's working class since at least the 1876 Centennial (though precursors go much further back, into the seventeenth century). It became an official city event in 1901. Neighborhood-based Mummers Associations prepare for months, lavishing attention on their costumes and movable sets. This stagecraft is at its apex in the legendary Fancy Brigades, who choose a theme each year and then compete in a judged pageant.

The Mummers Parade is an exuberant portrait of Philadelphia, in its full breadth (this year, there was even a costume based on Isaiah Zagar's famed Magic Gardens, pronounced by the *Inquirer* as "the most Philly thing ever").[2]

And this has long been true. The city's Swedish population played an important role in introducing the Mummers Parade, while Italian immigrants contributed many of its most baroque embellishments. It has since involved many other ethnic communities and also has inflamed controversy, through its tradition of blackface performance and other abusive caricatures. African Americans were explicitly excluded until the 1960s. Just in the past few years, though, Mummers have been working actively to address the issue. (In a memorably self-referential moment from 2017, a Donald Trump impersonator stripped to his underwear to reveal a sign reading "Flunked Sensitivity Training.")[3] New groups like Second 2 None, an African American drill team from West Philadelphia; the all-LGBT Miss Fancy Brigade; San Mateo Carnaveleros, a Mexican group; and South by Southeast, who represent the Asian community, have all recently joined the proceedings. This shift is itself the continuation of an ongoing tradition. As Thora Jacobson, a community arts leader who has served as a parade judge, notes, despite its sometimes troubled relationship with diversity, "the Mummers have always been a way of immigrant groups to find their way into society."[4]

Jacobson, as it happens, has also long been affiliated with another of the city's most prominent emblematic craft practices: the Mural Arts movement. This inspiring initiative, equal parts aesthetics and ethics, is not typically considered as part of the Philadelphia "craft scene." Yet, it has thrived only through a combination of expert skill and community support, just like all crafts. Subject matter for most of the murals is developed, as Jacobson puts it, "out of the mouths of the people who live nearby." And though professional artists design the imagery and oversee the execution, most of the actual painting is done by local residents.

Originally, this artistic workforce was drawn from the ranks of Philadelphia's graffiti culture—which, depending on your perspective, is either a public nuisance to the city or another of its thriving folk arts. Already in 1971, the Philadelphia Museum of Art began a mural program through its Department of Urban Outreach (later renamed the Department of Community Programs), working with prominent artists such as the painter Sam Gilliam. Later, under Mayor Wilson Goode, graffiti writers were asked to sign "the pledge," an agreement not to tag or deface walls, in exchange for amnesty from criminal prosecution. In 1984, the artist Jane Golden had recently returned to her home city from Los Angeles, which of course has its own vibrant mural tradition. Working closely with the Goode administration, she became the leader of the Philadelphia Anti-Graffiti Alliance (PAGN), which channeled creative energies into collaboratively achieved public artwork.

It has proved an extraordinarily fruitful strategy. Renamed the Mural Arts Program in 1996, the organization has created over 4,000 artworks under Golden's leadership. A technical breakthrough was achieved early on, at the suggestion of artist Kent Twitchell, who designed a huge mural of the basketball player Dr. J (1990), one of the program's first great successes. Instead of painting directly on the wall, the image was rendered on squares of "parachute cloth," a nonwoven polyester fabric. Using acrylic gel, the material can be attached to the side of a building without damaging it. This method not only has proved to be efficient and durable but also allows muralists to work on historic architecture.[5]

Tellingly, the subject matter of the murals often draws from Philadelphia's rich craft history, particularly the textile industry that flourished in the city beginning in the eighteenth century; quilts, African kente cloth, and even machine toolmaking have also appeared as motifs. In 2012, when the Center for Art in Wood opened its new location on Third Street in Old City, artist Benjamin Volta designed a mural for its north exterior wall. Featuring silhouettes of artworks in the center's collection, the mural was executed through the Restorative Justice Guild, a Mural Arts initiative that works with ex-offenders and probationers to create work readiness and reduce reincarceration.

The Mummers Parade and Mural Arts are clearly special cases. Yet, the success that both have found over the decades speaks volumes about Philadelphia's creative capital. Close enough to New York City to feel a sense of rivalry (but not close enough to be overshadowed), relatively affordable, and endowed with a rich legacy of industrial skills and settings, Philadelphia is well suited to grassroots, neighborhood-by-neighborhood inventiveness. This can be seen, too, in the proliferation of light manufacturing in the city. A few hardy companies survived the city's tougher economic years, like the metal manufacturer Amuneal, which was founded in 1965 but started making furniture only in 1998 and now runs a hip showroom on American Street in the postindustrial Kensington neighborhood, both for its own products and those of other small-scale manufacturers. There are also many new independent producers, often located in collaborative working spaces.

The high-end design firm BDDW, which makes wood and metal furniture, ceramics, rugs, and other goods, is often mentioned as a bellwether indicator. Under its charismatic leader Tyler Hays, who comes across as a combination of William Morris and Paul Bunyan, the twenty-five-year-old company has become a much-admired paradigm of strong design, fine craft, and adept marketing. Their showroom is in Manhattan and their factory is in Philadelphia, which says a lot about the two cities. BDDW's presence has also resulted in a sort of spin-off company, the lighting and furnishing firm

FINISHING A SLIPCAST CERAMIC MUG. *IMAGE COURTESY OF EDGEWOOD MADE*

Lostine; its founder Robert True Ogden has often collaborated with Hays and is one of the firms represented in the American Street Showroom.

John Pomp, based in Fishtown, is another prominent figure in this network of high-craft, low-volume manufacture. After studying glassblowing at Tyler School of Art, he went to New York City and established a network of retail clients. A decade later, he returned to Philadelphia and branched out into wood, metal, and leather, as well as his signature glass. Another cross-disciplinary company, Peg and Awl, is based in the Atlas Casket Factory— which still retains its historical conveyor belt and trolley track. Run by the

*Introduction — Glenn Adamson*

husband-and-wife team of Margaux and Walter Kent, the firm is explicitly romantic and nostalgic in its approach. They make extensive use of salvaged materials such as worn-out leather and wood from abandoned houses, trans-forming them into shoulder bags and furniture. On its website, Peg and Awl wears the city's identity as a historic craft capital like a slightly rusty badge: "We are makers. In Philadelphia. Still."

Among the new arrivals to this scene is Edgewood Made, whose proprietors, George Dubinsky and David Short, met during their studies at the Rochester Institute of Technology. When they resolved to set up their own craft-based batch manufacturing company, Philadelphia was an obvious choice, both

CNC-CUT-THROUGH TENONS. *IMAGE COURTESY OF EDGEWOOD MADE*

economically and symbolically. They first started out in ceramics manufacture and were initially attracted by The Clay Studio; today, having developed a line of wood furniture, they often cite Wharton Esherick as an inspiration.

After setting up shop in Kensington in 2013, they found that they did indeed have access to what they needed. Their workforce comes to them with training from the University of the Arts, or schools elsewhere in the Northeast. They have been able to acquire decades-old, heavy-duty woodworking machinery— so robustly built that it was still operational and extremely cheap thanks to the effects of globalization—and also have invested in a digital CNC (computer numerical control) cutter. They have found success on the trade show circuit and have now set up their own showroom in Lambertville, New Jersey. It's early days yet, but keeping up with sales is usually their biggest problem—the problem you want, as a new company—and their large shop gives them room to expand.[6]

One thing that may not be immediately obvious about such design-and-build firms is the degree to which they support one another. As Edgewood Made's David Short notes, many cities in America have inexpensive industrial build-ings to rent, but "Philadelphia's rich history in craft sets it apart. We could be in any city making things, but the more time I spend in Philadelphia, the more of a support structure I find."[7] And that structure is, again, very diverse. It includes companies ranging from Holzman Iron Studio, which spans a range from hand blacksmithing to 3-D modeling and engineering, to Maxwell Products, which uses economies of scale to make tools and equipment avail-able to a broad customer base (including BDDW). Alan Pyle, a salesman at Maxwell, observes that while traditional factories have left the Philadelphia area for good, they have been replaced by smaller firms—most of which have fewer than fifty employees (a cutoff point for certain government regulations).

Crucially, he says, "barriers to entry are low. If it's something that's in your blood, you can apprentice, then start your own business."[8]

On a whim, I asked Pyle if there were any bell makers still working in Philadelphia. It turns out there are. One of them is Malmark, located just outside Doylestown, north of the city. Founded by sound engineer Jacob Malta in 1973, the company is still going strong under the leadership of his daughters, Joanne Malta and Laura Moore. They specialize in musical hand bells for use by choirs. The work is mesmerizingly precise. It begins with nearby foundries, who sand-cast bronze bells to Malmark's specifications. These blanks are individually tested, then manually turned on a lathe to their final shape. In the process, fully 60 percent of the metal is removed (if a little too much is taken off, the bell must be discarded). This is highly skilled work, for each pitch of bell requires its own silhouette inside and out, with a variable wall thickness. The exact contours and alloy all have an effect on the pitch and tone. And tolerances are phenomenally tight: 43 percent of the bells are rejected at some point in the process.

Joanna Malta, like everyone else who makes things in Philadelphia, agrees that it is a perfect setting. Admittedly, her business is an unusual case. The city is, as she puts it, "bell-identified," and many of their sales are to clients with a historical interest. (In 1987, for the 200th anniversary of Pennsylvania's ratification of the US Constitution, Malmark provided bells to a choir drawn from the original thirteen colonies; they played wearing period dress.) But many of the variables that help make other firms are important for them too, especially the network of suppliers and the pool of talent. Nobody arrives at Malmark with the particular skills of bell tuning, but the company has always been able to attract and train the artisans they need.[9]

A five-story mural, a parade costume, a handmade table, and bells that play to perfection: all these things may seem very different. Yet, all of them, and much else besides, are being made in Philadelphia today. Craft connects the many neighborhoods and people of the city together; it is something Philadelphians hold in common. For centuries the city has been a center of skill, innovation, and community. That is still true. And whatever the future holds, one thing is certain: Philadelphia's craftspeople will be here, ringing the changes. ✬

*Notes*

1   This account of the bell's history is based in part on a groundbreaking technical study completed in the Bicentennial year of 1976: Victor F. Hanson et al., "The Liberty Bell: Composition of the Famous Failure," *American Scientist* 64, no. 6 (November–December 1976): 614–19. The original manufacturer of the Liberty Bell, Whitechapel Bell Foundry, went out of business in 2017 after 446 years in business.

2   Bethany Ao, "This Magic Gardens Mummers Suit May Be the Most Philly Thing Ever," *Philadelphia Inquirer*, December 20, 2018.

3   Allie Volpe, "How Do You Make A Parade Less Racist?," *The Outline*, January 2, 2017.

4   Quotations from Thora Jacobson are taken from an interview conducted on December 20, 2018.

5   For more on the history of Mural Arts, see Jane Golden and David Updike, *Philadelphia Mural Arts @ 30* (Philadelphia: Temple University Press, 2014).

6   Information on Edgewood Made is taken from an interview with George Dubinsky and David Short, conducted on November 16, 2018.

7   Email from David Short, November 16, 2018.

8   Interview with Alan Pyle, conducted on December 17, 2018.

9   Interview with Joanne Malta, conducted on December 17, 2018.

# MUMMERS PARADE

The Mummers Parade is a craft spectacular, and one of America's best-loved traditions of folk performance art. These images show the preparation of costumes by the Golden Sunrise New Year's Association, one of the city's historic "Fancy Brigades." They gather at a warehouse in South Philadelphia to create their costumes, often recycling components from past outfits. Many of the participants are family members who perform together.

PHOTOGRAPHS BY JESSICA KOURKOUNIS

# PHILADELPHIA'S CRAFT RENAISSANCE

*by*

*Sarah Archer*

In the May 14, 1967, issue of the *Philadelphia Inquirer*, art critic Victoria Donohoe described the Museum of Merchandise—an art exhibition disguised as a department store, organized by the Arts Council of the local YMCA/YWHA—as having "sufficient vigor and originality to project itself beyond a local audience." She added that "magazines and newspapers in other cities [had] given the art event advance coverage, probably because it is as restless and provocative a concept as anything seen in recent years."

**OPPOSITE | WOMAN IN COSTUME ON STAGE AT THE MUSEUM OF MERCHANDISE, 1967, FROM THE *EVENING BULLETIN*. AUDREY SABOL PAPERS, 1962–67. *ARCHIVES OF AMERICAN ART, SMITHSONIAN INSTITUTION***

The Museum of Merchandise brought together such wide-ranging characters as Andy Warhol and Roy Lichtenstein, who made silvered Coca Cola bottles and graphic black-and-white dishes, respectively, and Robert Arneson, who made ceramic flower pots for the store.[1] Robert Indiana designed a "LOVE" ring that took the form of his iconic outdoor sculpture, and Marisol designed a self-portrait ring, both of which were produced for the exhibition by the Rare Ring Co., one of the small companies in Villanova founded by Y Arts Council members Audrey Sabol and Joan Kron. They were also the proprietors of the Durable Dish Co., which made Lichtenstein's dinnerware, and the Beautiful Bag Co., which made canvas totes stenciled with Sabol's designs.[2]

Wound tightly into Donohoe's praise for the Museum of Merchandise is a quintessentially Philadelphian expression of cultural pride: people "out there" in the rest of the country (particularly a certain city that sits 94 miles due northeast) seemed genuinely *intrigued* by this exhibition, and not just in the way that visitors tend to offer a tourist's nodding acknowledgment of another Winslow Homer or Mary Cassatt show—events that just happen, like the turning of the fall leaves, or the annual Devon Horse Show. The Museum of Merchandise wasn't a richly storied but stuffy region simply doing what it does. It was the work of a new wave of Philadelphia art workers doing what Philadelphia historically *didn't* do: mix genres, turn accepted traditions upside down, offer wry critique, indicate a deep awareness of consumer and pop culture. It also embraced craft with quiet gusto. At this 1967 happening, a newly robust cohort of studio makers worked in collaboration with contemporary artists, fabricated from ceramics, textiles, and metal. The objects beckoned from the exhibition's faux department store shelves and were presented with no special explanation or conceptual asterisk.

How did Philadelphia's post–World War II studio craft renaissance take root, and why does it still flourish? One possible answer, suggested by the deeply intertwined relationship between traditional craft and high concept art at the Museum of Merchandise, is that Philadelphia grew into its avant-garde with craft practice at its fingertips.

One of the driving questions about Philadelphia's vibrant contemporary craft landscape—one so robust and layered that it seems like it must be a coordinated, centuries-long gift from previous generations—is why one of America's foremost industrial cities has nurtured a legacy of hand skill. How did Philadelphia's post–World War II studio craft renaissance take root, and why does it still flourish? One possible answer, suggested by the deeply intertwined relationship between traditional craft and high concept art at the Museum of Merchandise, is that Philadelphia grew into its avant-garde with craft practice at its fingertips.

Philadelphia acculturated early but embraced modernism late. Viewed through the lens of the city's current relationship with New York City, this makes sense: it's smaller, less monied, and somewhat less cosmopolitan. But in the colonial period, the reverse was true.[3] It was the country's capital between 1790 and 1800, and during that time, its spirit and style evinced an ancient Greek aesthetic. The city became home to new buildings that looked like ancient temples, locally made furniture that echoed the austere yet muscular forms of Europe's own neoclassical designs, and fashionable dresses that would not have looked out of place in antiquity.

GEORGE NAKASHIMA WITH HIS DAUGHTER, MIRA, IN HIS WORKSHOP, 1945.

*WAR RELOCATION AUTHORITY PHOTOGRAPHS OF JAPANESE AMERICAN EVACUATION AND RESETTLEMENT.*

*THE BANCROFT LIBRARY, UNIVERSITY OF CALIFORNIA, BERKELEY*

Democratic ideals were in the air, and forging new connections to a deeply rooted past allowed the citizens of this new country to project a kind of gravitas, following its revolutionary break with Great Britain. Franklin had wasted no time in bringing culture to his adopted city: he established the Library Company in 1731 and the American Philosophical Society in 1743. In the first decades of the nineteenth century, though the nation's capital had been moved south to Washington, DC, Philadelphia remained an epicenter of learning and culture, arts and fine craftsmanship, medicine and science.[4] The architects and designers who shaped the city at this time were enamored of the idea that Philadelphia (which had been given its Greek-derived name by William Penn) was the "Athens of America." The painter Gilbert Stuart described it this way, as did the architect Benjamin Henry Latrobe, who said he dreamed that "the days of Greece may be revived in the woods of America and Philadelphia become the Athens of the Western World."[5]

While craftsmen, many of them European born, produced furniture, clocks, musical instruments, ceramics, and silver for the city's growing patrician class, its civic leaders built schools and institutions of higher learning.[6] Local polymath Charles Willson Peale helped establish the Pennsylvania Academy of Fine Arts in 1805, the nation's first art school. The Philadelphia School of Design for Women (now the Moore College of Art & Design) was established in 1848 with the mandate of educating female designers for the city's robust textile industry. The city would go on to establish a reputation as a mecca for painting and sculpture both in academic and Impressionist modes. At the 1876 Centennial Exposition—at the dawn of the Gilded Age, nearing the height of Philadelphia's industrial powers—the charter was announced for the new Philadelphia Museum of Art.

Occupying 285 acres in Fairmount Park, the Centennial Exposition was the first official World's Fair in the United States, featuring displays from thirty-seven countries, and it attracted nearly ten million visitors. One of its most impressive structures, the Art Gallery designed by Herman J. Schwarzmann, is a Beaux Arts–style building now known as Memorial Hall. In the years following the fair, it reopened as the Pennsylvania Museum of Art and included the Pennsylvania Museum School of Industrial Art.[7] The School of Industrial Art (now the University of the Arts) was established following the 1876 Centennial in order to educate designers and craftsmen working in the metal, china, fabric, print, lighting, and furniture trades.[8] Inspired in part by the model of South Kensington in London, which similarly had its roots in the Great Exhibition of 1851, the School of Industrial Art was envisioned as a training ground for craftspeople whose talents would be needed in a fast-expanding economy. Just as the Victoria and Albert Museum was founded to better educate British designers and makers, Philadelphia's schools and museums were established as training grounds for the highly skilled and artistically talented. They did not set out to turn the art world on its head with radical new ideas, but to furnish the department stores, boutiques, and estates of the region's well-to-do. In need of additional space following growth and increasing attendance during the 1910s and '20s, the museum would eventually take its place on what has been described as an "Acropolis-like" hill on Fairmount on the banks of the Schuylkill River, where its Greek-inspired edifice has dominated the city's western skyline since 1928.

As a New World Athens, Philadelphia's civic and artistic leaders were not interested in mimicking its larger neighbor to the north; they were more enthusiastic about a sister city with deeper roots: London. Not unlike London, Philadelphia experienced a quiet craftsman revolution in its nearby rural counties in the closing decades of the nineteenth century, often in the shadow of manufacturing infrastructure. The Moravian Pottery and Tile Works was founded in 1898 by Henry Chapman Mercer, an archeologist and critic of American industrialization who apprenticed himself to a Pennsylvania German potter. Rose Valley was established in 1901 by architect Will Price on the land surrounding the defunct Rose Valley textile mill. Master metalsmith Samuel Yellin opened a studio and showroom in West Philadelphia in 1909. In neighboring New Jersey, the firms of Lenox China in Trenton and Fulper Pottery in Flemington enjoyed success well into the twentieth century.

At the same moment that Germany, France, the Netherlands, and the Soviet Union were breaking in modernism like a new pair of shoes, New York was experiencing the Harlem Renaissance and its own early forays into the avant-garde—the Museum of Modern Art (established 1929) and Jazz Age dance, theater, and music. Philadelphia was different. Less racially integrated and more traditional socially, some of its foremost cultural institutions were already 150 years old by the mid-twentieth century. Its orchestra gained a reputation for dazzling virtuosity under the leadership of Leopold Stokowski from 1912 to 1941, but it was not known for wild experimentation with new forms. The University of Pennsylvania's Institute for Contemporary Art was not founded until 1963 (just four years before the "Museum of Merchandise" opened its doors).[9]

So did Philadelphia simply lag behind? It may seem so, on the basis of the modernist bias that shapes so much of art-historical scholarship, and craft's long-suffering role as a conceptual distaff to contemporary art practice. Craft flourished in Philadelphia, one might suppose, because its art scene was behind the times. But turn this around: the postwar studio craft renaissance—which took place all over the world but took root with special firmness in the Delaware valley region—thrived here because it was the *form* that Philadelphia's avant-garde took.

By virtue of its modest scale, and its visual echoes of the feminine, handmade, homespun, or merely traditional, Philadelphia's postwar craft movement did not stun observers with its novelty the way contemporary art or modern dance did. Yet, its legacy *is* stunning: Philadelphia is not a wealthy city, but it remains home to an array of university craft programs that thrive even as other regions are cutting entire departments. Artists and small design firms have set up bustling studios in former textile mills, like the Globe Dye Works. And a constellation of nonprofit studios and residency programs, founded in the 1960s and '70s, are as busy and well funded as ever. Philadelphia craft may have seemed fairly ordinary in the 1950s, but it has been vital enough to bloom well into the twenty-first century.

Leading the charge through much of the movement's history has been the educator and gallerist Helen Drutt.[10] Having studied art history at Temple University and grown up in the city, Drutt describes her decision to establish her eponymous gallery in 1973 as a simple, practical necessity: the artists of the organization she had founded, the Philadelphia Council of Professional Craftsmen (PCPC), needed a permanent place in which to have exhibitions. In the 1950s, Drutt had begun to make visits to the studios of Phillip Lloyd Powell, Paul Evans, and Wharton Esherick in Bucks County, Pennsylvania.[11] In 1953, she purchased a "Nest" table from George Nakashima for $18. Through the courses she developed and taught at the Tyler School of Art in the history of craft, and the exhibitions she curated, she was both cultivating and documenting a contemporary craft movement that was unfolding in real time.

HELEN DRUTT IN HER GALLERY AT 1625 SPRUCE STREET, 1979

INSTALLATION AT HELEN DRUTT GALLERY, 1979, INCLUDING WORK BY RUDOLF STAFFEL, WAYNE HIGBY,

WILLIAM DALEY, LIZBETH STEWART, KAREN KARNES, AND JOHN GLICK

*Philadelphia's Craft Renaissance — Sarah Archer*

PAUL EVANS AND PHILIP LLOYD POWELL OUTSIDE THEIR SHOWROOM IN NEW HOPE, PENNSYLVANIA, CA. 1960.

*PHOTOGRAPH COURTESY OF DORSEY READING*

OPPOSITE

*WHARTON ESHERICK WITH OBLIVION, 1934, BY EMIL C. LUKS.*

*WHARTON ESHERICK MUSEUM COLLECTION*

*Philadelphia's Craft Renaissance — Sarah Archer*

During this period, Philadelphia's colleges were making consequential hires, particularly in ceramics and metalwork. At Tyler there was the jeweler and digital-design pioneer Stanley Lechtzin, and ceramist Rudolf Staffel, whose vessels in porcelain combined free handling of the material and transcendent luminosity. At the Philadelphia College of the Arts, Swedish-born Olaf Skoogfors taught metalsmithing until his untimely death at forty-five in 1975, and William Daley taught ceramics for four decades. At Arcadia University (then called Beaver College), Paula Winokur established the ceramics program. She and her husband, Robert, shared a studio in Norristown, Pennsylvania, until her death in 2018. Drutt came to know all these makers; she frequented Makler Gallery on South 18th Street and purchased her first ceramics by Daley and Staffel at Gallery 1015 in Wyncote.

During this time, Drutt met a Baptist minister named Richard M. Jones (at a lecture at the University of Pennsylvania delivered by Marshall McLuhan, no less). Jones shared Drutt's sense that the city could benefit in myriad ways from an entity that represented the serious craft artists of the region, setting them apart from hobbyists. They aimed to give the general public a more nuanced understanding of craft, in part by advocating for more exhibition opportunities at local museums and university galleries. Jones encouraged Drutt to spearhead the project. A first meeting took place at Lechtzin's home, with Dan Jackson, Richard Rinehart, Daley, and Skoogfors in attendance. It was here that Drutt first saw a brooch by Lechtzin and was bowled over by its original form. "Ornament was ready," she has said, recalling the excitement of the potential "to take gigantic leaps into the world of art."[12] In 1973, after six years of organizing PCPC exhibitions in Philadelphia and across the country, including Daley's first solo show at the Art Alliance in 1969, and an exhibition of new work by David Watkins and Wendy Ramshaw at the AIA in 1973, Drutt

*FROM LEFT*, METALSMITHS EARL KRENTZIN, RONALD HAYES PEARSON, PHILLIP FIKE, OLAF SKOOGFORS, AND STANLEY LECHTZIN, WITH LECHTZIN'S ELECTROFORMING EQUIPMENT, AT THE 1964 SYMPOSIUM ON METALS AT THE FIRST WORLD CONGRESS OF CRAFTSMEN. *PHOTO: © ACC*

STANLEY LECHTZIN IN THE JEWELRY STUDIO ON THE ELKINS PARK CAMPUS, IN TYLER HALL, 1989. *PHOTO: ROBERT E. DIAS, TEMPLE UNIVERSITY LIBRARIES' SPECIAL COLLECTIONS*

established her own gallery on Spruce Street. Philadelphia quickly became a hub in the global jewelry network.

A heightened sense of Philadelphia craft's special vibrancy and originality inspired the Women's Committee at the Philadelphia Museum of Art to establish the museum's annual Contemporary Craft Show, now entering its forty-third year. In 1965, the committee had made its first foray into retail fundraising efforts by opening an Art Sales and Rental Gallery at the museum, known for a time as ArtWorks, where it hosted a contemporary jewelry sale called "A Touch of Gold" in 1974.[13] The Craft Show began in 1977 and was the first of its kind—other museums, including the Museum of Arts and Design in New York and the Smithsonian in Washington, DC, have established juried craft shows of their own. The PMA Craft Show is consequential for the museum in several ways. Its proceeds support the acquisition of an important studio craft object for the permanent collection each year. It also connects Philadelphia to sister cities with robust craft communities around the world through its annual Guest Artist program, which, since 2001, has brought artists from Europe, Africa, Asia, and the Middle East to exhibit their work at the show.[14]

Equally important was the 1970 formation of Collab, initially called Inter-Society Committee for Twentieth-Century Decorative Arts and Design, the Philadelphia Museum of Art's affinity group for modern and contemporary design. Though not a craft advocacy group per se (the affinity group Techne fills that role), Collab was established at a high point in Philadelphia's craft output. It was conceived by interior designer and Women's Committee member Cynthia Drayton working in collaboration with the museum's director, Evan Turner, and curator, Calvin Hathaway. In 1968, Drayton had assisted Hathaway in the acquisition of a silver decanter made by Olaf Skoogfors, which then inspired her to wonder why the museum was not acquiring more work by

Philadelphia's master makers. Collab was the result. With its early corps of members composed largely of architects and interior designers, there was a natural emphasis on furniture. Early in its existence, the Pennsylvania chapter of the National Society of Interior Design donated a 3107 stacking chair and Egg armchair and ottoman by Arne Jacobsen. The American Institute of Architects donated a lounge chair by Charles and Ray Eames. But there were other important early craft gifts, too: the National Home Fashions League donated work by Philadelphia ceramists Paula Winokur and Rudolf Staffel and glass artist Roland Jahn.[15]

Philadelphia's academic and gallery craft scenes were complemented by a grassroots studio movement composed largely of recent graduates of the area's many art schools, and a more accessible retail landscape of shops and studio sales. In 1965, Ruth Snyderman founded the Works Gallery with a

*CLAY/PAPER*, EXHIBITION AT SNYDERMAN WORKS GALLERY, 1979, INCLUDING WORKS BY
ROB SIEMINSKI (*FOREGROUND*), SUSAN LANGE (*WALL MOUNTED*), AND MARTHA GITTLEMAN AND
MICHAEL OLIJNYK (*REAR WALL CASE*).

partner in Rittenhouse Square, one of the city's most well-heeled neighbor-hoods. Offering an alternative to department stores full of mass-market home goods, Snyderman's shop catered to a clientele that craved handmade and stylish things to use and admire. In 1970 Ruth and her husband, Rick, moved the gallery to South Street, just as the area was experiencing a renaissance. There were ten craft shops in the neighborhood, as well as the experimental Theater of the Living Arts. At South Street they attracted an enthusiastic and bohemian clientele. The Snydermans worked with local artists Julia and Isaiah Zagar and potter Vickie Gold to establish the Head House Open Air Market, working with architect Richard Saul Wurman to design the space. The market featured craft artists selling their wares, alongside stalls offering various ethnic cuisines—precursors, perhaps, to today's Art Star Craft Bazaar with its varied array of food trucks.[16]

In 1974, a group of five recent ceramic graduates decided they needed a dedicated studio space, and the organization now known as the Clay Studio was born. Cofounder Janice Merendino recalls that at that moment—the year she graduated from Moore College of Art & Design—"my options as a ceramic student were to either continue at a university or find space on my own."

Artists who study in Philadelphia or come here to establish a studio have centuries of history to thank for the conditions that make it such an attractive city for creative workers.

Having selected a physical location in Old City that was too big for the five of them, the group essentially guaranteed that others would follow. Fellow cofounder Jill Bonovitz notes that Philadelphia was a prime place for this sort of organization because of the concentration of art schools and the pioneering work of Drutt.

During the same period, brothers Albert and Alan LeCoff were, improbably, operating the entity that would eventually become the Center for Art in Wood out of Albert's home in Germantown, initially calling itself the Wood Turning Center and opening in 1986. Both LeCoff brothers were fascinated by the long history of the John Grass Wood Turning Company, which operated in Old City (across the street from the current location of the Clay Studio) starting in 1863; by connecting across generations of technique and style through a combination of research, architectural salvage, and creative work, Alan and Albert LeCoff epitomized the Philadelphia craft revival: rooted in history and open to an artistically ambitious future.[17]

Artists who study in Philadelphia or come here to establish a studio have centuries of history to thank for the conditions that make it such an attractive city for creative workers. Philadelphia deindustrialized in the postwar period but managed to hold on to and support its great museums, even as art schools primed it to become a seedbed of craft activity. What it has retained, as its industrial output has waned, is its concentration of art schools, many of which still have strong craft curricula, both for students of art history and budding makers (or both). Its constellation of craft-focused nonprofits offers makers educational and retail opportunities, and places to exhibit. Sometimes they even drive the city's evolving urban plan. The Fabric Workshop and Museum, founded by Marion Boulton "Kippy" Stroud in 1977, launched its program by inviting leading contemporary artists to experiment with fabric and textiles in a large industrial building on the edge of Chinatown. The Clay Studio, which has been in Old City for four decades, will move in 2020 to the newly vibrant neighborhood of South Kensington.

And the city's former industrial life has left behind an architectural gift: a landscape rich in buildings that are ideally suited to artists' studios and small-batch production. Sometimes, as in the case of the former Globe Dye Works in the city's northeastern corner, or the Bok Building, a former technical high school in South Philadelphia, they're large enough to house scores of tenants, creating a brand-new creative community as artists put down roots. In these shared spaces, a visit can feel magical, because the mix is likely to include metalsmiths, furniture makers, potters, milliners, neon artists, and fashion designers working alongside coffee roasters, independent record labels, bike shops, printers, photographers, and florists. It's hard to discern where one category ends and another begins. This agility has largely saved Philadelphia from the postindustrial fate of smaller Rust Belt towns in the Northeast and Midwest, and that of cities that lacked Philadelphia's deeply sunk roots, educational and cultural. Its economic ebbs and flows have helped fashion it into a place where creative workers can find affordable space to work, teach, experiment artistically, and live well. This encourages the making of creative work that can be, but doesn't have to be, commercially viable in a particular mode, at a particular moment—or even comprehensible to the casual observer. Or, it can inspire artists to make work that's magnanimously accessible at an array of price points, inviting a wide swath of the population to share in the local cultural treasures. By evolution rather than design, it seems to be a model that works. Or to paraphrase Victoria Donohoe, writing in 1967: "as restless and provocative a concept as anything seen in recent years." ✯

## Notes

1   Marina Pacini, "Who but the Arts Council," *Archives of American Art Journal* 27, no. 4 (1987): 9–23.

2   Wendy Weitman, *Pop Impressions Europe/USA: Prints and Multiples from the Museum of Modern Art* (New York: Museum of Modern Art, 2002), 129.

3   Ira Berlin, "Slavery, Freedom, and Philadelphia's Struggle for Brotherly Love, 1685–1861," in Richard S. Newman and James Mueller, eds., *Antislavery and Abolition in Philadelphia: Emancipation and the Long Struggle for Racial Justice in the City of Brotherly Love* (Baton Rouge: Louisiana State University Press, 2011), 22.

4   Alexandra Alevizatos Kirtley, "The Athens of America," in *The Encyclopedia of Greater Philadelphia* (online).

5   Kirtley, "The Athens of America."

6   David Jaffee, *A New Nation of Goods: The Material Culture of Early America* (Philadelphia: University of Pennsylvania Press, 2011), 259.

7   Linda P. Gross and Theresa R. Snyder, *Philadelphia's 1876 Centennial Exhibition* (Mount Pleasant, SC: Arcadia, 2005), 105.

8   The University of the Arts was known from 1964 to 1985 as the Philadelphia College of Art, or PCA.

9   Darrel Sewell, ed., *Philadelphia: Three Centuries of American Art; Bicentennial Exhibition, April 11–October 10, 1976* (Philadelphia: Philadelphia Museum of Art, 1976), xxii.

10  This passage is informed by an unpublished chronology assembled by Helen Drutt. The author and editor thank Drutt for access to this and related research materials.

11  Oral history with Helen Williams Drutt English, July 5–October 20, 1991, Archives of American Art, Smithsonian Institution, 68.

12  Joyce Lovelace, "Mobile and Movable," *American Craft Magazine*, September 2013.

13  "The Women's Committee of the Philadelphia Museum of Art," https://twcpma.org/about/history/, accessed December 26, 2018.

14  "The Philadelphia Museum of Art Contemporary Craft Show," www.pmacraftshow.org/about-the-show#history, accessed December 26, 2018.

15  Kathryn Hiesinger, *Collecting Modern: Design at the Philadelphia Museum of Art since 1876* (New Haven, CT: Yale University Press, 2001), 145.

16  Ruth and Rick Snyderman, "A Brief History of Craft in Philadelphia," unpublished manuscript, April 2015.

17  Old City became one of Philadelphia's major craft corridors in the early 1990s, when the Snydermans established a gallery on Cherry Street, and Robert Aibel opened Moderne Gallery, which specializes in the work of studio makers such as George and Mira Nakashima and David Ebner.

# SIMON FIRTH

Simon Firth started his involvement with cycling as a bike messenger in the 1980s in London. After coming to Philadelphia in 1995, he got his first job at VIA bikes, then continued on to work for master frame builder Stephen Bilenky. After fifteen years Simon started his own brand, Hanford Cycles, specializing in handmade steel bicycles. He works out of a shop located inside the store he co-owns, Firth & Wilson Transport Cycles.

PHOTOGRAPHS BY JESSICA KOURKOUNIS

# CRAFTING A COLLECTION

*by*

Elisabeth Agro

Contemporary craft was integral to the founding mission of the Philadelphia Museum of Art (PMA) and remains so today. The curatorial work I perform behind the scenes is changing the very essence of my institution. ✯ When it was founded in 1876, the Pennsylvania Museum and School of Industrial Art (as it was then called) differentiated itself from other fledgling institutions in Hartford, Boston, Chicago, and New York by assembling a collection of decorative arts, initially with acquisitions from the 1876 Centennial Exposition.

OPPOSITE | EXTERIOR OF THE PERELMAN BUILDING WITH A YARN BOMB BY JESSE HEMMONS (ISHKNITS) DURING *CRAFT SPOKEN HERE*, 2012, *PHILADELPHIA MUSEUM OF ART LIBRARY & ARCHIVES*

Modeling itself after the Victoria and Albert Museum (V&A) in London, the PMA focused on exceptional examples of decorative arts, made by hand or machine, both historical and modern.

Despite these beginnings, in 1945, director Fiske Kimball noted that the collections lacked representation of twentieth-century decorative arts. The Board of Trustees showed little interest in the applied arts, though occasional gifts of contemporary craft and design, such as Swedish glass and hand-wrought pewter, were sporadically received. In 1945, the museum purchased four works by renowned ceramists Gertrud and Otto Natzler, another instance of an isolated acquisition. In retrospect this purchase was foundational. These works were the first examples of American studio craft to enter the museum's collection, just at the genesis of the movement itself.

GERTRUD AND OTTO NATZLER, BOWL, 1945. EARTHENWARE WITH VERT DE LUNE GLAZE.

*PHILADELPHIA MUSEUM OF ART, GIFT OF MRS. HERBERT CAMERON MORRIS, 1945*

GERTRUD AND OTTO NATZLER, VASE, 1943. GLAZED EARTHENWARE WITH SILVER-GREEN GLAZE.

*PHILADELPHIA MUSEUM OF ART, GIFT OF MRS. HERBERT CAMERON MORRIS, 1945*

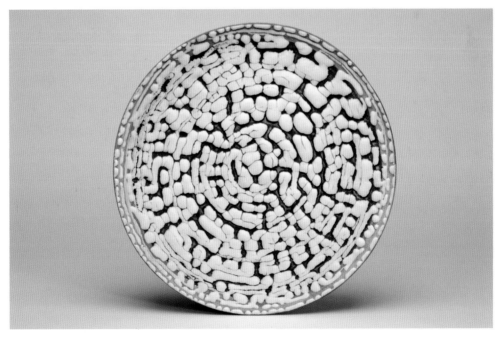

GERTRUD AND OTTO NATZLER, PLATE, 1941. EARTHENWARE WITH WHITE ORNAMENTAL GLAZE.

*PHILADELPHIA MUSEUM OF ART, GIFT OF MRS. HERBERT CAMERON MORRIS, 1945*

*Crafting a Collection — Elisabeth Agro*

The 1970s was a pivotal decade for contemporary craft at the museum. The year 1970 saw the formation of the Inter-Society Committee for 20th-Century Decorative Arts and Design (now known as Collab), a volunteer group dedicated to supporting the museum's decorative art and design collections. This was likely in response to an expanded focus on craft at Philadelphia's notable art schools, the convergence of talented artists, and the proliferation of galleries and emergence of steely, focused advocates at the center of an extremely vibrant scene that gained national attention. The creation of the American Art department in 1971 and the hiring of Darrel Sewell, the Robert L. McNeil Curator of American Art, in 1973 permitted the museum to fully participate in this transformation. Sewell, trained as a curator of paintings, took a serious interest in craft and added it to his curatorial purview. This was no flight of fancy; he pursued key acquisitions such as Wendell Castle's *Music Stand* (1972), William Daley's *Floor Pot* (1974), and Robert Arneson's *David* (1977) within his first four years at the museum. This effort was strengthened in 1977, when the Women's Committee of the PMA launched its annual craft show as a fundraiser. By 1981, the committee dedicated a percentage of the proceeds to the acquisition of contemporary craft, permitting the museum to acquire steadily in all craft media ever since.

Following Sewell's retirement in 2002, Robert L. McNeil Jr., a trustee and chair of the American Art Committee, made a transformative gift to endow the first curatorship in the United States dedicated to modern and contemporary craft. (The position was named for his wife, Nancy M. McNeil, cofounder of the Philadelphia Craft Show.) Appointed to the post in 2006 by Director Anne d'Harnoncourt, I was charged to engage colleagues across departments in a dialogue about craft in an international context. This mission fostered energetic professional discourse, a growth in acquisitions, an increase of installations in the museum's galleries, and a series of special exhibitions focusing on craft in a global context.

During my first week on the job, d'Harnoncourt expressed to me her wish that I enmesh myself within the craft community, regionally, nationally, and internationally. She also gave me my first assignment, four years down the road: an exhibition in conjunction with the 2010 Philadelphia National Council on Education for the Ceramic Arts (NCECA) conference. The result of this directive was *Interactions in Clay: Contemporary Explorations of the Collection*. I commissioned four artists—Walter McConnell, Paul Sacaridiz, Ann Agee, and the late Betty Woodman—to create site-specific work influenced by our historic collections and period rooms. It was a first for the museum to place contemporary art into these stagnant historical settings; the period rooms never looked better!

In 2008, d'Harnoncourt unexpectedly passed away, but I remained dedicated to her charge to connect to the craft community, both within and beyond Philadelphia. It was a new era; social media was exploding. With my colleague from the West Coast, Namita Wiggers, I founded Critical Craft Forum (CCF), a platform on Facebook for dialogue and exchange. It took off, beginning with just under 200 members when we launched in 2009, and now numbering over 11,000 members from every corner of the world. CCF also hosts sessions at College Art Association, providing another means for our community to connect virtually and academically.

Donors Leonard and Norma Klorfine followed McNeil's lead by establishing a dedicated fund for contemporary craft in 2008, which supports programs, research, exhibitions, and acquisitions. Over the past thirteen years, the collection has grown exponentially—in fact, it has doubled. It didn't take me

ANN AGEE'S INSTALLATION IN *INTERACTIONS IN CLAY*, 2010.

*PHILADELPHIA MUSEUM OF ART LIBRARY AND ARCHIVES*

*Crafting a Collection — Elisabeth Agro*

long to realize that I should be in the business of collecting contemporary masterpieces: works that can hold their own alongside art made in their time but also connect with art that is centuries old.

Timothy Rub, who became director in 2009, ushered in a new focus at the PMA on art that finds itself on the fringes, outside the canon. My collections were suddenly not to be relegated to hallways and byways. A gap in the exhibition schedule produced an opportunity: *Craft Spoken Here* (2012), the first major exhibition of this collection. CraftLAB, an educational and community program placed within the exhibition, and our Yarn Bombing of our building's entrance, reinforced that craft is critical to the museum's charge. The project also paved the way for an installation series titled *At the Center: Masters of American Craft*, featuring prominent artists from the Philadelphia region. Importantly, these five exhibitions were installed in our permanent American Art galleries in the main building. I secretly feel that I fired a cannonball across mainstream art's bow!

For the past decade, I have avoided the Sisyphean question: Is craft art? To me, the very need for my curatorial position says it all. So, I focus on the collection in everything I do; how I write, speak, install, and think. The object is primary. This informs two aspects of my work, which to the initiated are inextricably linked. The first, the classification of artwork, is often dismissed as a rote and onerous task. How an object is cataloged will determine how it is found, including online, and therefore how it is perceived, and even its position in future art history. The metadata becomes forever intertwined with the object, like DNA. Good cataloging is truly a love letter to the future. We need to get excited about this work. It will establish connections we cannot even fathom. This does not take away the unique and special way we speak, write, and talk about craft. It only adds more to what we have to say. It permits others who are not familiar with our field to gain access, thereby including us in the mainstream conversation. I recognize that we are in an age where the blurring of categories is celebrated—we respect "crossover" artists and we should. I also respect self-designation. But it is imperative we define and classify; in doing so we understand what we are blending, where we came from, and where we are going.

Keeping my eye on the marketplace to maintain and build the collection is another aspect that holds primacy in my work. The fate of craft collections now in private hands is a concern, a hot topic, and is the gorilla in the room that collectors, gallerists, the auction houses, and curators have been unwilling to discuss. Newsflash: there is no plan. A large percentage of the work is undocumented and unpublished, even for artists who are our icons. With each passing year, the number of collections going to auction increases. Like a tsunami, the first waves have already hit the shoreline. Some objects hold their own; many are sold for much less than their value. Many others are "bought in," garnering no bids or falling short of the reserve price to be left unsold. I was recently told that scrappers are showing up at the smaller auction houses to buy up studio jewelry made of precious material, only to melt it down. I am sounding the bell. If you are not alarmed, you should be!

In my daily work I try to make inroads to these challenges, both in public and unseen ways. I liken it to a rock thrown in a still lake, resulting in those gentle ripples that radiate beyond. Craft today is prominent, due to the confluence of a myriad of eclectic artists from around the world, with energies from academia, commercial, and public institutions. As a guardian of the galleries at the PMA, I am playing my role in the craft economy. The question that I'll leave you with is this: What is yours? ⭐

CRAFT SPOKEN HERE, 2012. PHILADELPHIA MUSEUM OF ART LIBRARY AND ARCHIVES

*Crafting a Collection — Elisabeth Agro*

# MARTHA McDONALD

Martha McDonald makes performances and installations that feature
handcrafted costumes and objects, which she activates through movement
and song. Her practice often focuses on site-specific interventions that uncover
hidden narratives of a site. She has developed work in historic-house museums,
botanic gardens, a Victorian cemetery, a construction waste-recycling facility,
and a small boat journeying down a river.

PHOTOGRAPHS BY JESSICA KOURKOUNIS

*by*

*Chad Curtis*

# Over the past decade, 3-D modeling on the computer and digital fabrication—3-D printing, CNC machining, laser cutting—have become standard practice in many craft programs. While now common across the globe, the use of this technology in the studio arts originated in Philadelphia at the Tyler School of Art, Temple University, in the Metals, Jewelry, and CAD-CAM (MJCC) program in the 1980s.

OPPOSITE | TYLER SCHRANDT, *TRANSPOSE*, 2018. PRINTED CLAY, INSULATION FOAM, PALLET WOOD.

At the heart of this innovation was Stanley Lechtzin, who founded the MJCC program in 1962 (see photo on p. 47). His studio work is known for his innovative use of technology and materials, often drawn from industrial processes. Lechtzin's digital work evolved through three primary phases, beginning with a variation on the electroforming process that allowed him to create large-scale, lightweight jewelry in an unconventional manner (he patented the process in 1982).[1] He then investigated the creative potential of plastics, celebrating their transparency and vibrant color palette, while largely abandoning the use of metal conventional to the medium. Finally, in what now seems a logical development of this work, Lechtzin embraced the use of computer-aided design and computer-aided manufacturing (CAD-CAM) technology.

The MJCC program offered its first official computer-aided design and computer-aided manufacturing class in 1989, well ahead of other craft (or fine art) programs.[2] When Lechtzin was honored with the Lifetime Achievement Award in 2009 by the Society of North American Goldsmiths, Matthew Hollern wrote: "Stanley Lechtzin has been a preeminent figure responsible for the adaptation, adoption, and advancement of new technologies."[3]

Nearly three decades after this first CAD-CAM class at Tyler School of Art, the use of digital fabrication, as it is now often called, is nearly ubiquitous in art, craft, and design education. However, this spirit of innovation has continued at Tyler and, more broadly, in Philadelphia. The rapidly declining cost of the technology has also allowed it to make its way into community-oriented makerspaces such as NextFab in Philadelphia, and personal studios. Coupled with this affordability, accessibility is being driven by commercialized digital-fabrication tools. These systems are simpler to use, are more reliable, and are able to produce durable, high-resolution objects.

The MJCC program offered its first official computer-aided design and computer-aided manufacturing class in 1989, well ahead of other craft (or fine art) programs.

Building on Lechtzin's legacy, I introduced digital fabrication in the Ceramics Program at the Tyler School of Art in 2011, affording students the opportunity to be the among the first in the country to use this technology with clay. Tyler Schrandt, who graduated from the MFA program in ceramics in 2018, made full use of these tools in his thesis research. Drawing on algorithmic design and 3-D printing directly in clay, his work explores the intersection of craft, design, sculpture, and installation. Schrandt examines the evolving forms of labor that he, as a self-defined craftsperson, invests in his work while also addressing his longing for a deeper understanding of an increasingly digital world. For him, digital fabrication is both a means to an end and a vehicle for personal and cultural reflection.

My own work has explored the intersection of digital fabrication and craft-based practice for over a decade, both in my studio and in teaching. *Wondering about Mars* is a project that utilizes images from NASA's Mars Reconnaissance Orbiter to digitally fabricate plaster molds. From these molds emerge terra-cotta tiles that reproduce and make tactile the Martian landscape, in a material that is literally of the earth. It is experienced in a physical manner not possible in an image. More broadly, I am invested in considering how we know and understand our world beyond our immediate experience, and the ways that digital technology both facilitates and inhabits that experience. In practice, this question literally plays out in my studio as I move between handmade and digital means of production.

CHAD CURTIS, *WONDERING ABOUT MARS*, 2016. INSTALLATION VIEW.

Doug Bucci, an alumnus of the MFA program in MJCC and a beneficiary of learning digital fabrication as a student in the late '90s, recently joined us at Tyler as the interim program head, following Lechzin's retirement. Much of Bucci's work draws on his experience as a diabetic, using data derived from his wearable continuous glucose-monitoring system, connected to an insulin pump, to generate nontraditional jewelry. In his Islet series, Bucci uses the diabetic cell structure as a building block for the forms, which are then altered by data—reflecting the chemistry of his blood—retrieved from his medical devices. Digital technology is not only a vehicle for him to generate form, but also a means to reveal the most personal of information. Jewelry, by its nature, shares that information with a public audience.

Rashida Ng and Andrew Wit, faculty in the Architecture Department at the Tyler School of Art, and Dr. Tonia Hsieh, faculty in the Biology Department at Temple University, are collaborating to utilize digital modeling and physical prototyping to address climate change and deforestation in Costa Rica. Their project—cloudMAGNET—is a series of carbon-fiber kite forms intended to fly above the rainforest. As air passes through a series of Venturi tubes incorporated into the kites, the air pressure is locally altered and results in the formation of small rain clouds, which potentially could help reverse the effects of deforestation.[4] While still a speculative proposal, this research relies on several forms of digital and conceptual modeling, both in form generation and in creating computational fluid dynamic (CFD) simulations. However, when generating their kite prototypes, they draw on a manual process remi-niscent of fiber art from the 1970s, winding the carbon fiber filament around a jig prior to curing the forms with heat in a kiln. It is a fascinating project that marries the high tech with some of the oldest craft traditions to address urgent environmental concerns.

DOUG BUCCI, *TRANS-HEMATOPOIETIC | BLACK, NECKPIECE*, 2011. RESIN PRINTED AS ONE INTERLINKED PIECE.

RASHIDA NG + ANDREW JOHN WIT, *CLOUD MAGNET*, 2018. 1/4-SCALE PROTOTYPE.

As the tools become more accessible and easier to use, and the novelty factor wears thin, these examples provide a way forward; digital fabrication does not need to be simply a means to an end. These examples are by no means comprehensive, and there are many more people within the field of ceramics using this technology in ways that are equally generative and experimental. The craft disciplines have a long history of makers that have an intimate relationship both with their tools and materials. Lechtzin's own trajectory as a craftsperson is an excellent example and provided a foundation for others at Tyler to build on. ✰

## Notes

1   Stanley Lechtzin, patent, "Method of Electroforming and Product," August 10, 1982.

2   Douglas Bucci and Matthew Hollern, "Influence of the Digital: Context and Form," *Metalsmith* 25, no. 3 (2005): 36–43.

3   Matthew Hollern, "2009 Archive—Society of North American Goldsmiths," paper presented at Society of North American Goldsmiths conference, June 15, 2009, www.snagmetalsmith.org/2009/.

4   Rashida Ng, Andrew Wit, and Tonia Hsieh, "Cloud Magnet: The Ethical Imperative for Environmental Health and Restoration," in *Happiness: The Built Environment Shaping the Quality of Life; Proceedings of the ARCC-EAAE International Conference, Philadelphia, May 16–19, 2018*, ed. Kate Wingert-Playdon and Hazem Rashed-Ali, 20–28 (Philadelphia: Architectural Research Centers Consortium, 2018).

# MATT SAUNDERS

Matt Saunders is a scenic designer and
creator of new performance work based
in Philadelphia. A founding member and
associate artistic director of the experimental-
theater company New Paradise Laboratories,
Saunders has designed over 150 works of
theater, opera, and live performance. His
work has been presented in Philadelphia at
the Walnut Street Theatre, the Arden Theatre
Company, the Headlong Dance Theater, the
Pig Iron Theatre Company, Theatre Exile,
and the Wilma Theater.

PHOTOGRAPHS BY JESSICA KOURKOUNIS

**"WHEN SUN COMES OUT"**

LETUMI
LP 2777
VOL.III

Featuring:
"SUN RA on PIANO"
AND
"JOHN GILMORE on TENOR SAX"   "The SUN RA ARKESTRA Leaves Planet Earth"

by

Anthony Elms

# You don't just waltz into a different world. Passageways need to be forged. I've always been attracted to those who draw passages out.

They see more in willing an alternative here; they desire more in wanting an alternative here. My alternate history of Philadelphia craft begins fully formed in 1968, with the arrival of Sun Ra and his Arkestra to the Germantown neighborhood. Ra knew a thing or two about other worlds: religious, musical, humorous, disciplined, racialized, linguistic, and, of course, cosmic.

OPPOSITE & OVERLEAF | *SUN RA IMAGES COURTESY OF JOHN CORBETT*. COLLECTION OF THE ALTON ABRAHAM COLLECTION OF SUN RA, UNIVERSITY OF CHICAGO LIBRARY.

He wanted his visions to have authority and do business—in practical terms, to release albums of his music and volumes of poetry and promote the band. But his plans neither started nor stopped there. An undated and unsigned document outlines the aims:

> Purpose: To performs [*sic*] works of a humanitarian nature among all people of Earth, to help stamp out ignorance destroying its major purpose, to own and operate all kinds of research laboratories, studios, electronic equipment, and electromechanical equipment, electronic equipment related to audio and video devices and audio and video devices themselves including sound recordings and tapes as well as video recordings, tapes, teleportation, astral projection devices, mind cleansing sound devices, magnetic computers, electrical and electronic devices related to all phases of enterplanetary space travel, including space ships with speeds beyond the speed of light, including enterplanetary cosmonetic devices of an astro infinity nature, to own real estate and all other factors related to real estate including, land, buildings, water, including air space above same, to use these values for the advancement of all people of Earth . . .[1]

With incorporation he made this range legit. What has always impressed me about Sun Ra isn't his far-out performances and pronouncements, but the everyday present-tense physicality of his expansive vision. Most noticeable were the costumes—sequined, shimmering, and spacey. And handprinted album covers, painstakingly drawn on assorted papers and films, converted into printing plates and block stamped, published in batches from a dozen or so into the hundreds. Also business cards. Everything under the guise of doing business. His own business.

# "ART FORMS OF DIMENSIONS TOMORROW"

SATURN ® ©1965

# SUN RA and his Solar Arkestra

## FEATURING

JOHN GILMORE
MARSHALL ALLEN
PAT PATRICK
RONNIE BOYKINS
CLIFFORD JARVIS
ALI HASSAN
JIMHMI JOHNSON
CLIFFORD THORNTON
JOHN ORE
SCOBY STROMAN
MANNY SMITH

**THE POTENTIAL**

Beyond other thoughts and other worlds
are the things that seem not to be
And yet are:
How impossible is the impossible,
Yet the impossible is a thought
And every thought is real
An idea, a flash of potent fire
A seed that can bring to be
The reality of itself.
Beyond other thoughts and other worlds
Are the potentials...
That hidden circumstance
And pretentious chance
Cannot control.

**THE SHADOW OF THE FIRE**

The vibrations of the sounds seem the same
But the meaning of the sounds
Take separate directions
At the crossroads
of the Cosmic-point of the arrow . . .
Beyond this Age
Through the darkness of the light years
And the light years of the darkness
Is the pure light of the pure darkness
And the pure darkness of the pure light.
The light is as the darkness
Because the light is the image
And the shadow of the fire.

Sun Ra

### SIDE A

I CLUSTER OF GALAXIES
Sun Harp, Spiral Percussion Gong.....Sun Ra; Thunder Drums.....
Pat Patrick, Tommy Hunter;

II ANKH
Trombone Solo.....Ali Hassan; Piano Solo.....Sun Ra; Baritone Sax
Solo.....Pat Patrick; Tenor Sax.....John Gilmore; Percussion.....
C. Scoby Stroman; Alto.....Marshall Allen; Bass.....Ronnie Boykins

III SOLAR DRUMS
Sun Harp, Piano, Dragon Drum.....Sun Ra; Space Drums.....John
Gilmore; Bells.....Marshall Allen; Percussion.....C. Scoby Stroman;
Bass.....Ronnie Boykins

IV THE OUTER HEAVENS
Tenor Solo.....John Gilmore; Alto Solo.....Marshall Allen; Trumpet
Solo.....Manny Smith; Clarinet Solo.....Pat Patrick; Bass.....Ron-
nie Boykins; Piano Solo.....Sun Ra

### SIDE B

I INFINITY OF THE UNIVERSE
Piano, Percussion Solo.....Sun Ra; Percussion.....Clifford Jarvis;
Dragon Drum, Bass Clarinet.....John Gilmore; Trumpet.....Clifford
Thornton; Bass.....Ronnie Boykins; Drum.....Pat Patrick; Sticks,
Drum.....Marshall Allen

II LIGHTS ON A SATELLITE
Piano Solo.....Sun Ra; Tenor Solo.....John Gilmore; Bass.....John
Ore; Percussion.....C. Scoby Stroman; Baritone.....Pat Patrick;
Bass.....Ronnie Boykins

III KOSMOS IN BLUE
Piano Solo.....Sun Ra; Tenor Solo.....John Gilmore; Bass — 1st
Solo.....Ronnie Boykins; Bass — 2nd Solo.....John Ore; Percussion
.....C. Scoby Stroman

Cosmic-Equations
POEMS
and
COVER DESIGN
by
SUN RA

SATURN RECORDS
P.O. BOX 7124
CHICAGO 7, ILLINOIS
U.S.A.

MUSIC Composed and arranged by SUN RA.
Published by Interplanetary (BMI)
Copyright © 1965

LP No. 9956
Stereo
Solar-Fidelity

SUN RA IMAGES COURTESY OF JOHN CORBETT. COLLECTION OF THE ALTON ABRAHAM COLLECTION OF SUN RA,

UNIVERSITY OF CHICAGO LIBRARY

Anyone can dream. Harder is to build an otherwise dreamworld with your hands. Ra built one in which he was a myth from Saturn, and music was the guiding superstructure and transport. That world did business with ours. We can still visit the receipts and invoices. During his lifetime, every chuckle or dismissal in response to Ra proclaiming himself beyond earthly limits was cunningly refuted, one long-playing record at a time. If governments and social spheres would not confer the proper authority upon Ra and his people, he crafted for himself and those he cared for a splendidly regal authority of their own devising. He wove these scintillating threads into the frayed gray flannel of everyday life.

Fast forward some decades, to thesis five from poet Lisa Robertson's "26 Theses on Craft (Bordélique)":

> Pleasure is only apolitical to those who have never been subject to its willed and policed historical foreclosure. The diversification of pleasure as aesthetics, by means of convivial bodily effervescence of form, is part of the necessary politics of the present. One of craft's uses is to decorate. Decoration is memory externalized. Whose décor shall we inhabit? Perhaps now, rather than less, we need more decoration, but of our own devising, as homeopathic antidote to the ubiquitous mass-produced décor called information.[2]

When I think craft in Philadelphia, I think along these lines. I think of a number of artists who do not make solitary objects. I think of those, like Ra, who have walled off the givens of context, to handbuild new conditions and communities; who have limited the authority of the here and now, to bring us more-worthwhile relationships with pasts and futures; who could have stopped at solid material but instead move into messier, otherwise gatherings.

A short list could include—yes, the still-functioning Arkestra, now under the guidance of longtime member Marshall Allen—also Karen Kilimnik, who has evolved from the scattershot violence and awed staging of her early installations to plush rooms incorporating luscious draped fabrics, tart videos, giddy collages, and romantic paintings: dreamy historical non-places that lull us into joyful, nearly louche, resplendent recline. And Virgil Marti, who meticulously and beautifully metallicizes ornaments in arrangement, highlighting a death mask or period vase, say, accented in delicate poofs and baroque curvatures, setting solemn collections up for tomorrow's bricolaged embrace. And the something's-just-off-from-center-gravity mystic/domestic chambers—both miniature and life-size—for paintings and ceramics by Joy Feasley and Paul Swenbeck. Or the fierce polyrhythmic time cuts undertaken by Black Quantum Futurism (Camae Ayewa and Rasheedah Phillips) via events, situations, and publications, to unwrite Eurocentric, colonial, and white supremacist meters of present and future.

This list is cruelly abbreviated. None of these makers are necessarily innovative in their forms. But they recognize how tuned groupings of gesture—big, small, incongruent—can keep the overwhelming crush of indistinctive information and as-is settings at bay. All their works involve carefully crafted attention to space, decor, and matter. This is how they draw a boundary against our bureaucratic everyday. They invite us with them at close-enough proximity to slip into something convivial to new pleasures.

One last fellow traveler: artist Alex Da Corte. He has slow shifted; once there were distinct sculptures and videos. Also shelves, retail strategies, cheeky signage, the softened rub of carpet, and paneling. Then other artists' actual objects started creeping in at the edges, as ghostly re-creations, caddish repurposings, and tender homages to other art forms. Then the videos grew

VIRGIL MARTI, INSTALLATION OF *FOREST PARK* AT LOCKS GALLERY, PHILADELPHIA, 2014.

*COURTESY OF THE ARTIST AND LOCKS GALLERY*

OVERLEAF

ALEX DA CORTE, *RUBBER PENCIL DEVIL*, 2018. ALUMINUM, NEON, RUBBER, AUTOMOTIVE PAINT, VELVET,

GLASS, VINYL, FOAM, HARDWARE, PLEXIGLAS, PLYWOOD, SPEAKERS, MONITORS, FOLDING CHAIRS,

HD DIGITAL VIDEO. *PHOTO: TOM LITTLE*

*Other Planes of Here — Anthony Elms*

rooms. And collaborations spilled authorship in all directions. Rooms became house sized, took on ambiance and scents. Da Corte didn't cross media; he added media, to make safe environments to give private desire a social scale. His work doesn't alienate, yet it does oppose the definitions of attraction often housed through window and screen.

From an unpublished proposal by Da Corte:

> I have been thinking of our nation's ethos, the American Dream. It is a funny combination of words. Does it imply achievement in America equals existing on a plane separate from Reality? Live in a dream. My sole hope in life was to be an animator. After many turns in the road, I guess I am an animator, or re-animator. I make work with late capitalist consumer objects—the good and bad goods the American Dream is made of. I cobble them together, in the spirit of Dr. Frankenstein, and give them new life.[3]

If your politics are under threat—if, as is true for so many, your desire for subjecthood, or feeling for objecthood, is yet to be given due process—it isn't enough to make an object for someone else. You must cobble together your worlds. That is something all the abovementioned have touched. "How do you make an American quilt?," Da Corte asks. "It takes many hands. It is shared. It is all of our concern. You cannot keep yourself warm with a picture of a quilt."[4]

This diversification of aesthetic pleasure is part of a necessary politics for any present, a force against the willed and policed foreclosures of marginalized freedoms and desires. This politics needs to ornament to oppose the status quo. To change the framing of a room, or the mannerisms of writing; to part lush curtains for a warming reveal; to tantalizingly fringe those now gone; to sew the sweep of your sequins to Saturn. All this changes your role. Give Da Corte the last word on this reality: "If you place enough holes in a bucket, you will have a net."[5] ✮

## Notes

1    This unattributed document can be seen in John Corbett, Anthony Elms, and Terri Kapsalis, eds., *Pathways to Unknown Worlds: Sun Ra, El Saturn and Chicago's Afro-Futurist Underground, 1954–68* (Chicago: WhiteWalls, 2007), 98.

2    Lisa Robertson, "26 Theses on Craft (Bordélique)," reprinted in *F. R. David*, Autumn 2018 (Glasgow and Berlin: uh books / KW Institute for Contemporary Art, 2018), 16.

3    Alex Da Corte, "Herb 2," unpublished document, unpaginated.

4    Ibid.

5    Ibid.

rock urban
management

(215) 964 9039

A RECENT INSTALLATION BY PHILLY-BASED STREET ARTIST
EPHEMEROH, WHO CAPTIONED A PHOTO OF IT WITH "A FENCE,
STEEL SLATS, OR 'WHATEVER YOU WANT TO CALL IT.'" —DJT
IN AN OBVIOUS REFERENCE TO A WALL ALONG THE MEXICO
BORDER, EPHEMEROH HAS PLACED A LADDER OVER IT.

# STREET ART

Although many people associate the emergence of graffiti with New York City in the 1980s, street art actually began in Philadelphia in 1967, when Darryl McCray began painting his tag "Cornbread" across the city. Philadelphia remains not only a creative territory for new local street artists, but also a destination for others worldwide.

PHOTOGRAPHS BY JESSICA KOURKOUNIS

BALTIMORE-BASED ARTIST REED BMORE IS KNOWN FOR HIS WIRE SCULPTURES AND HAS BEGUN
HANGING THEM FROM ELECTRICAL WIRES IN PHILADELPHIA OVER THE PAST COUPLE OF YEARS.

THE GRAFFITI WALL AT FIFTH AND CECIL B. MOORE IS A STREET ART ICON. IT IS WHAT IS CALLED A "PERMISSION WALL," AND THE OWNERS GIVE STREET ARTISTS FREE REIN. THE WALL, WHICH IS REALLY THREE WALLS, HAS BEEN PAINTED CONTINUALLY SINCE THE '80S, CHANGING CONSTANTLY AS ONE MURAL PIECE GETS COVERED BY ANOTHER AND SO ON. THIS IS ABOUT TO END, SINCE THE PROPERTY HAS BEEN SOLD TO A DEVELOPER. THERE IS WHAT APPEARS TO BE A POP-UP BEER GARDEN GOING IN, WITH FENCING SURROUNDING IT THAT WILL CONTINUE TO OPERATE AS A CANVAS FOR STREET ART.

GRAFFITI PIER—CONSIDERED AN UNSANCTIONED STREET ART MUSEUM. THE PROPERTY IS A PIER AND PARCEL OF LAND ON THE DELAWARE RIVER, FORMERLY PART OF THE READING RAILROADS AND THE PORT RICHMOND YARDS. IT WAS ABANDONED IN 1991, ALTHOUGH IT'S STILL CONSIDERED PRIVATE PROPERTY BECAUSE IT'S OWNED BY CONRAIL.

# MAKING SPACE(S) FOR CRAFT

*by*

Michelle Millar Fisher

On a chill February Thursday, as the Eagles led their jubilant Super Bowl victory parade through the city, I became Philadelphia's newest resident. (The moving company almost canceled on me because they were concerned about entering the city, so large was the predicted celebration.) Now over a year later, I'm settling in well—right at the moment when the city is blossoming. There is a widening recognition of superlative food joints at every price point and persuasion—believe the hype around Barbacoa and swear by the soup at the Good Spoon Soupery.

OPPOSITE | THE BOK BUILDING. *PHOTO: SAM OBERTER*

Community support swells for progressive mayor Jim Kenney and District Attorney Larry Krasner, who are focused on social-justice initiatives, and public satisfaction abounds in the freeing from a contested incarceration of hometown rapper Meek Mill. *GQ* named Philadelphia their City of the Year for 2018. A city famed for its underdog status has flipped the script. As *GQ* staff writer (and Germantown native) Zach Baron reflected, "To be from Philadelphia is to be accustomed to losing . . . we were the nation's capital, until we weren't. . . . But then a weird thing happened: We started winning."

Journalists at men's style magazines may be forgiven, just, for not knowing that when it comes to craft, architecture, and design, Philadelphia has *always* been winning. Architecture is a special point of pride here. Although Boston's MIT likes to claim credit, this city witnessed the first structured classes on architecture, taught under George Strickland in 1834. It was the setting for Louis Kahn's elegiac midcentury sermons on materiality. A central locus of postmodernism, Robert Venturi's house for his mother, Vanna, was built here. Scottish transplant Iain McHarg birthed the modern landscape architecture movement here, and Laurie Olin keeps that flame burning still.

However, as I learn Philadelphia's contemporary design and craft scene not from books but on the ground, one studio and institutional visit at a time, I recognize the importance of a different kind of architecture and infrastructure. The current efflorescence of makers in Philadelphia is predicated upon the ability to work in affordable studios (and to return at night to affordable homes). More often than not, these workspaces are located within historic architecture, which has been adapted to provide creative havens and hubs of collaborative exchange.

The first such threshold I crossed was Lindsey Scannapieco's renovated Edward W. Bok Technical High School, now known as the Bok Building, in South Philadelphia. Hulking over a full city block, it was designed in an imposing art deco style by city architect Irwin Catharine as a Public Works Administration project in 1938. The building was listed on the National

G. FARREL KELLUM WORKING IN A STUDIO AT THE BOK BUILDING. *PHOTO: MICHAEL PERSICO*

*Making Space(s) for Craft — Michelle Millar Fisher*

The wood shops, culinary training kitchens, science labs, and classrooms that once hosted students learning crafts are now home to jewelers, architects, furniture makers, fashion designers, milliners, and product designers.

A WORKSHOP AT THE BOK BUILDING. *PHOTO: MICHAEL PERSICO*

*Craft Capital: Philadelphia's Cultures of Making*

Register of Historic Places in 1986, but the vocational school within closed in 2013. Scannapieco and her team have thoughtfully repurposed its existing facilities to serve the needs of individual makers, small businesses, nonprofits, and small-batch manufacturers. Painfully aware of the delicate balance between creating a creative hub and building a monster of gentrification, the project's leaders are rightfully proud that 80 percent of the building's tenants are South Philly residents. The wood shops, culinary training kitchens, science labs, and classrooms that once hosted students learning crafts are now home to jewelers, architects, furniture makers, fashion designers, milliners, and product designers. (There are also charitable organizations, a daycare, and even a local boxing club.) Only a quarter of its 340,000 square feet of space has been repurposed to date; the project's a long-term labor of love. Home to over fifty craft and textile artists, as well as more-esoteric specialties such as medical-device manufacturers, the 1241 Carpenter Studios, which I stumbled upon next, are located in the Hawthorne neighborhood, bordering South Philly; the nineteenth-century factory building used to be the Main Belting Company. Blacksmith Louise Pezzi and fabric installation artist Kay Healy are among notable residents, while the owner, Steven Krupnick, is an inventor and maker.

A facility called MaKen, housed within two industrial buildings from the 1910s—a former textile factory and the headquarters of the now-shuttered Richardson Mint Company—similarly provides spaces for rent to artists and manufacturers, but in the north of the city. Its motto, "Made in Kensington, the workshop of the world," is an umbrella for diverse studios, including furniture makers, ceramicists, a handmade lingerie maker, an ice cream kitchen, and a body-positive boudoir photographer. Just a few minutes farther north is Globe Dye Works, which was also once part of the textile trade, dyeing and winding yarn from the 1860s onward. Globe Development Group took the buildings over in 2007 with the mission to convert them into affordable studios, and to build a

MAKEN NORTH STUDIO. *IMAGE COURTESY OF SHIFT CAPITAL*

*Making Space(s) for Craft — Michelle Millar Fisher*

community of like-minded practitioners. The latter goal is appropriate to the history of this space, and of others like it, since it was customary for mill owners to lease parts of their production floor to related industries. (In the later nineteenth century, Globe Dye Works had five tenants, including cotton goods companies Steadfast Mills and Garsed Bros., who produced towels, ginghams, miner's flannel, as well as Willow Brook Hosiery.)

Located to the south, in Fishtown (like Kensington, a neighborhood shaped by heavy industry), Crane Arts is housed in the cast-concrete and brick-faced Crane Company Building. Built in 1905 and designed by Philadelphia architect Walter Ballinger, the Crane building was initially used as a plumbing warehouse and then to process frozen seafood. A concrete block added to its first floor, once a giant freezer, is now the Ice Box Project Space for interdisciplinary exhibitions. Crane Arts, too, bursts at its seams with studio, exhibition, and nonprofit creative offices. The late (and beloved) Nicholas Kripal, a long-standing ceramics professor at Tyler University—where he worked for four decades—bought the Crane Building in 2004 with his retirement savings as a stable studio environment for artists and makers, safe from the precarities of rapid gentrification.

It is no hyperbole to say that you can *feel* energy radiating from buildings like these and pulsing outward through the city. I'm not the person to ask whether it's always been this way, but Philadelphia feels like another proud underdog that I know and love: my hometown of Glasgow. Each was once a bustling center of shipbuilding and textile manufacture during the long Industrial Revolution, and both cities have been unwillingly—and often unfairly— overshadowed by nearby metropolises (Edinburgh and New York). In the last half century, the creative capital in both places has played a crucial role in reasserting identity and remaking economies after deindustrialization

It is no hyperbole to say that you can *feel* energy radiating from buildings like these and pulsing outward through the city. I'm not the person to ask whether it's always been this way, but Philadelphia feels like another proud underdog that I know and love: my hometown of Glasgow.

wreaked its path. I can still remember, at seven years old, marveling as teams of men turned streaky black to coral red as they blasted centuries of grime off the sandstone facades of tenement buildings, in anticipation of Glasgow's status as European City of Culture in 1990.

The remaking of places like Bok, 1241 Carpenter Studios, MaKen, Globe, and Crane are part of a similar renaissance in Philadelphia. It gives me hope that their developers, and those who occupy their studios, continue to sport the small chip on their shoulders. It is what makes both cities so special. Ultimately, it is what will keep both of them open, accessible, and creatively rich, and filled with residents who are fiercely proud to live and make there. ✬

# JUDITH SCHAECHTER

Judith Schaechter is a stained-glass artist who has lived and worked in Philadelphia since 1983. Her pieces often use symbolism from the history of her discipline, particularly the height of stained glass in the medieval Gothic era. But the distorted faces and figures in her work have been likened to twentieth-century German expressionist painting, and her subject matter is entirely secular. Schaechter teaches at University of the Arts and conducts frequent workshops to share her skills.

PHOTOGRAPHS BY JESSICA KOURKOUNIS

*by*

*Don Miller*

# Philadelphia is a remarkable environment in which to contemplate and make craft. Historical spaces and artifacts permeate the present as nowhere else in the country. An awareness of the cultural past, and perhaps its influence as "prelude," is inescapable.

The wealth of historical institutions caters to the popular imagination, lending to daily-life temporal diversity and spatial texture. The sensibilities and creative imaginations of craft artists, especially, are quickened in this rich environment.

OPPOSITE | KARYN OLIVIER, *THE BATTLE IS JOINED*, 2017. VERNON PARK, GERMANTOWN. *PHOTO: STEVE WEINIK*

The city surprises with treasures of material culture at every turn. The ghosts of generations of woodworkers, metalsmiths, and potters are our invisible companions as we make our work among the shops in which they labored. Craft genres themselves—unceasing and continuous cultures of making— are manifest in our day-to-day surroundings.

Germantown, a working-class neighborhood in Philly's northwest, borders the ravines of Fairmount Park. Initially settled by the Lenape tribe and, later, German Mennonite farmers, the area became a locale for the summer villas of wealthy Philadelphians and was the site of an important Revolutionary War battle. This historical identity permeates Germantown's present-day character. Eighteenth-century homes line its main artery, interspersed with the storefront churches, salons, and row houses typical of working-class Philadelphia. Hundreds of artists work in a wealth of affordable space. Imperfect Gallery, a neighborhood institution, thrives, not on sales of contemporary art but on the devotion and support of a diverse arts community.

In this environment, collisions between past and present are frequent, yet always poignant and surprising. History progressing at its own unknowable slow pace can overwhelm the contemporary. The overgrown church burial grounds are crowded with epitaphs. Ruined industry is slowly reclaimed by nature in the empty lots and woods. The formal rooms of villas are continually transformed by light and shadow. Time is experienced as duration, as *becoming*.

Time is an essential consideration to craft practitioners; it could even be thought of as our primary material. Craft culture is often identified by outcomes—the quality and function of objects—but inspiration, motivation, and ideas are, more often, found in our involvement with social and natural histories. Craft reflects the continual evolution of work in depth in a chosen material. Even more importantly, practitioners "make" the time that we experience through that creation.

These thoughts bring to mind the work of local artists who have explored this neighborhood for the possibilities that time offers both as motivation and material. I look to their work for a diverse and deep articulation and affirmation of shared values.

For many in Philadelphia, Germantown is indelibly associated with the woodworker and educator Daniel Jackson—an important yet largely unacknowledged progenitor of the studio furniture movement. He helped define a genre that melds historical decorative art with contemporary sculpture. His work celebrated and built on the carving traditions for which Germantown had long been known. Jackson lived and worked in the neighborhood during a period of social unrest that dramatically transformed its economic and cultural fabric. I can only imagine his reaction to this cataclysm: the bittersweet disappearance of a slow, deep culture of making and his efforts to preserve its depth. To find solace. His spirit inhabits this neighborhood still, a kindred spirit spanning the ages, and, for me, an everyday partner in the workshop.

*The Battle Is Joined*, by the Germantown sculptor Karen Olivier, was installed in Vernon Park in 2017. The work encases a nineteenth-century monument to a Revolutionary War battle in mirror, literally reflecting the natural environment and, more figuratively, an expanse of time. The distant historical event, obscure and almost without context, is made manifest by rendering it nearly invisible. Static monumental history is replaced by an image of ongoing seasonal transformation, metaphorically implying an unceasing struggle for freedom.

In my own life and work, I've always searched the everyday past for present meaning, a sense of origin. As a child I dug for treasure, evidence of my forebears. And I made stuff. Always made stuff.

Bill Gerhard's work also embodies fleeting temporality. He first records the imprints of Germantown rain on wet plaster. After it dries, he uses it as a casting mold. Through this simple process, Gerhard captures the slow patterns and processes of nature—a reprieve from the distracted perceptual time frame we've come to accept as normal. Each material has its own distinct quality: the permanence of bronze, the sense of industrial ruin that pervades aluminum, and the uncanny mimesis of glass, which appears to preserve the raindrops intact. These works compress the vastness of time into human scale with sensual intimacy. Looking at Gerhard's work closely, I am reminded of the words of Henri Focillon, who saw art as the secret labor of nature at the heart of human invention, "fluid and imponderable."

In my own life and work, I've always searched the everyday past for present meaning, a sense of origin. As a child I dug for treasure, evidence of my forebears. And I made stuff. Always made stuff. My choice to study instrument making—my first craft—was sparked by a desire to imbue materials with their own life. I share this with fellow craftspeople. I believe it to be basic, essential to the need to make.

*Elizabeth* is not a piece inspired by or based on an idea. A simple stone in a neighborhood burial ground clung to my eye and gestated for months. The piece started as a replica of that stone, a simple copy that I hoped would lead somewhere unexpected. Making a copy, if approached with humility and critical curiosity, sometimes helps reveal the truest character of an object.

A FINDING IN GERMANTOWN. *PHOTO: DON MILLER*

Replicating the stone's basic scale and shape, a carved elliptical hollow serves as a focus for formal contemplation. As I neared carving the inscription, I wondered, Who was Elizabeth? How can I connect with her, "make" the distance in time into something tangible, intimate? Intuitively, I reversed the name as if viewing it backward through the solidity of material. I view the work as a concrete poem that gives form to time, memorializing a long-deceased neighbor and new friend.

Several weeks ago, I was walking up Tulpehocken Street on a trash day. A double-take backed me up. Upon a nineteenth-century carriage step was propped an iridescent purple cushion from some awful sofa. Music to my eyes! The gentility of old Germantown. The crassness of contemporary disposable consumer culture. The time and space between collapsed. Once again, I was moved, a bit bewildered but ultimately galvanized by the chasm of time that lurks beneath the surface of daily life in Germantown—an intimate reminder, an affirmation, of the perpetual renewal of craft culture. ✭

WILLIAM GERHARD, *UNTITLED (4-16-18)*, 2018. RAIN-PITTED PLASTER CAST IN ALUMINUM AND GLASS.

*COURTESY OF THE ARTIST AND MAGGIE PINKE*

*Crafting Time — Don Miller*

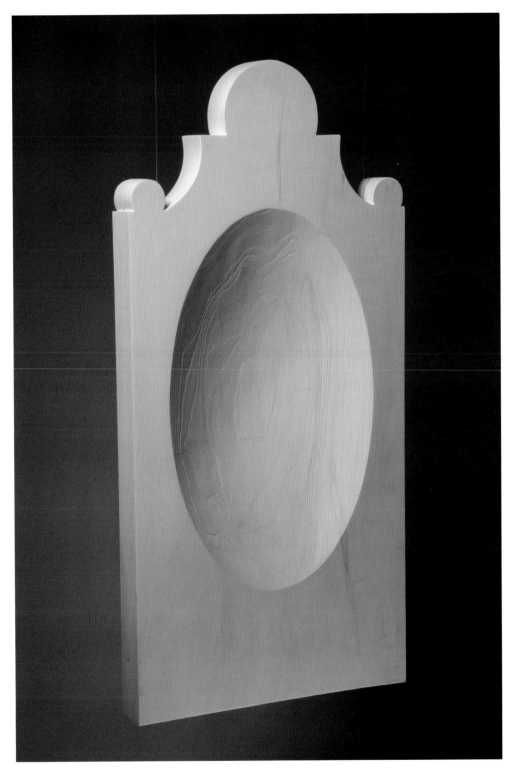

DON MILLER, *ELIZABETH*, 2013. BLEACHED MAPLE. *PHOTO: KEN YANOVIAK*

*Crafting Time — Don Miller*

# CHRIS DiPINTO

In 1992, Chris DiPinto began re-creating 1960s pawn-shop-style guitars by hand. Rather than building exact copies, he has incorporated modern techniques and added upgraded hardware so that the guitars played like modern, well-made instruments. In doing so, he helped bring about the birth of the modern-retro guitar that is so popular today. DiPinto has made guitars for Los Straitjackets, the Cars, Cheap Trick, Jack White, and David Bowie and still sells instruments through his guitar store in Fishtown.

PHOTOGRAPHS BY JESSICA KOURKOUNIS

# CRAFTING COLLABORATIONS

*by*

Jennifer-Navva Milliken

## "Collaboration" is a messy concept that defies neat classification.

It can be interpreted in myriad ways, from the pragmatic to the social and idealistic. Artist cooperatives, makerspaces, and coworking studios offer the exchange of skills, tools, muscle, and space. Collaborations also take the form of invitational events and artist residencies, which host artists in focused studio-based interactions. Ultimately they result in cross-disciplinary projects that are expansive in character, methodology, and scope. Artists and makers in Philadelphia are exploring the potential of all these models.

OPPOSITE | CRISTINA TAMAREZ, *JANINE AND MICHAEL*, ITE 2018.
BLACK-AND-WHITE 35 MM FILM NEGATIVE, SCANNED.

Particularly vibrant is the culture of collaboration in the woodworking field, which takes place against a backdrop of over three hundred years of industrial wood turning, fine cabinetmaking, and artisanal furniture production. Though Philadelphia's historical workshops may seem distant when compared to today's participatory ways of working, the city's extensive history of woodworking provides a fertile foundation on which to build.

A case in point is the Windgate International Turning Exchange (ITE), organized by the Center for Art in Wood. This residency program enfolds "collaboration" into its tripartite mission of "research, exploration, and collaboration."[1] In the words of the center's cofounder, Albert LeCoff, "This collaboration mirrored their historical relationship in which turners made the elements—back spindles, legs, and rails—that furniture makers incorporated into their chairs."[2] Each year, the ITE hosts artists from around the world for eight weeks of focused art-making, reflection, and study in a communal environment. Now approaching its twenty-fifth year, the program greatly influences the center and its operations, most tangibly in its collection of artworks, to which residents have characteristically donated a work of art created on-site. Unsurprisingly, many of these works embody the spirit of collaboration and the ITE program's intimate living and working conditions; this may take the form of group-made assemblages that serve as documents of a time and place, while bearing the distinctive "signatures" of participating artists. Other artists have had more-protracted dialogues, as seen in Todd Hoyer and Hayley Smith's *Untitled #1*, created during their residency in 1995. In this case the collaboration also became a personal union, in the marriage of Hoyer and Smith.[3]

THE RESIDENTS OF THE WINDGATE INTERNATIONAL TURNING EXCHANGE IN 2009, AT THE UNIVERSITY

OF THE ARTS, PHILADELPHIA. *PHOTO: ROBERT LYON*

TODD HOYER AND HALEY SMITH, *UNTITLED #1*. MADE AT THE WINDGATE INTERNATIONAL TURNING EXCHANGE

(ITE), 1995. ASH. THE CENTER FOR ART IN WOOD MUSEUM COLLECTION, DONATED BY THE ARTISTS.

1995.09.01.005. *PHOTO: JOHN CARLANO*

A number of other community-building events serving artists in wood emerged concurrently with the Windgate ITE program. Among them is the annual Echo Lake Conference at Bucks County Community College. Echo Lake is modeled on a biannual event held at Emma Lake (hence the name) in Saskatchewan, Canada, and is supported in part by the Bucks County Woodturners. Taking place over a period of three and a half days, Echo Lake is an invitational event that hosts artists (the majority of whom specialize in woodworking, furniture making, or metalsmithing) in a nonstop festival of creating and communing. The legendary intensity of the conference is mitigated by a focus on play and spontaneous interaction, as makers are released from the usual constraints of studio production work. Echo Lake also nurtures exchanges between two disciplines, wood and metal, which involve processes that invite unrehearsed and responsive making to take place between participating artists.

Philadelphia also has seen the rise of permanent collaborative spaces, such as coworking studios and cooperative workshops. These give artists and makers the convenience and access of working in an urban environment, without the high costs of operating a solo workshop in the city. For Philadelphia furniture maker Rachel Fuld, the advantages of working in a group environment include seasoned advice, extra sets of skilled hands, and simple camaraderie—often missed by artists who work in isolation.[4] Michael Vogel, who founded Philadelphia Woodworks, likens the experience of working in a cooperative space to working out in a members' gym. Although there is an inherent difference between cooperating on a project and working side by side on independent projects, he believes that sharing space and expertise results in a greater sense of community responsibility and conscientiousness.[5]

Philadelphia is also home to multidisciplinary arts collectives, which use collaborative models as a way for artists and makers to share not only space and equipment, but also ideas and inspiration. Many are founded by cohorts of graduates, who find themselves armed with ideas, motivation, and brand-new academic degrees, but no access to a studio or equipment at the standards they experienced in school. By combining their resources, emerging artists can establish workshops that allow them to work independently, while preserving the sense of community that comes with studying in a program. One such cooperative, Traction Company, is home to a diverse group of member-makers. They share not only facilities, but also professional opportunities and commissions. There is a chain effect of opportunity exchange—one project leads to another. Members also show their work together in organized exhibitions.

A recent initiative, *PHL Assembled*, involved the participation of various Traction Company members. The citywide event included an exhibition at the Philadelphia Museum of Art, as well as citywide actions, meetings, performances, lectures, and artist-made objects and structures, all geared toward civic engagement. In many ways, *PHL Assembled* resembles the proposal-driven performance and public art movement of the 1960s; then as now, artists called for the removal of barriers between makers and viewers and rejected the rarefied spaces of museums and galleries. Collaborative on a mass scale, *PHL Assembled* continues to be active in urban space and online, and it issues manifestos for tackling systemic issues that plague the city.

SHELDON ABBA, MOBILE SANCTUARY DOME, TRACTION COMPANY, PHL ASSEMBLED, PHILADELPHIA, 2017.

35 MM FILM NEGATIVE, SCANNED.

*Craft Capital: Philadelphia's Cultures of Making*

Cumulatively, collaborative models may also be influencing the city's commercial furniture companies. One of the most prominent of these, BDDW, aims to achieve "a different experience of how to be in the world and make furniture."[6] Committed to the long-term employment of local artists and designers, it brings a high level of craftsmanship to process-driven design and operates in a shared open space. This workshop environment seems reminiscent of the small-scale manufacturing companies—such as the John Grass Wood Turning Company[7]—that earned Philadelphia its reputation as a "Workshop of the World."[8] ✯

## Notes

1    Albert LeCoff, "The Launching of the International Turning Exchange," in *Connections: International Turning Exchange, 1995–2005*, ed. Judson Randall (Philadelphia: Wood Turning Center, 2005), 6.

2    Ibid., 10.

3    Tanya Harrod, "The Artist in Residence: A Sketch," in *Connections: International Turning Exchange, 1995–2005*, ed. Judson Randall (Philadelphia: Wood Turning Center, 2005), 46.

4    From a telephone conversation with Rachel Fuld, dated November 20, 2018.

5    From a telephone conversation with Michael Vogel, dated November 20, 2018.

6    Conversation with Fuld.

7    The John Grass Wood Turning Company (1863–2003) was an industrial outfit that produced turned-wood objects for industrial and household use. Established by German émigré John Grass in Philadelphia's Old City neighborhood, the company operated in its space at 146 N. 2nd Street. For more information, see https://centerforartinwood. org/johngrass/content/construction-today-john-grass-sp08.pdf.

8    See *Invisible Philadelphia: Community through Voluntary Organizations*, eds. Jean Barth Toll and Mildred S. Gilliam (Philadelphia: Atwater Kent Museum, 1995).

# MICHAEL HURWITZ & MAMI KATO

Married couple Michael Hurwitz and Mami Kato share conjoining studios in Fishtown, northeast of central Philadelphia. The building is entirely devoted to artists' studios. Hurwitz, one of America's finest studio furniture makers, had made his home in the city for thirty years, initially to head the woodworking program at the Philadelphia College of Art (PCA), now the University of the Arts. Kato attended PCA during these years as a student, studying sculpture. In the past decade, she has developed a unique body of work involving an unusual material, rice straw.

PHOTOGRAPHS BY JESSICA KOURKOUNIS

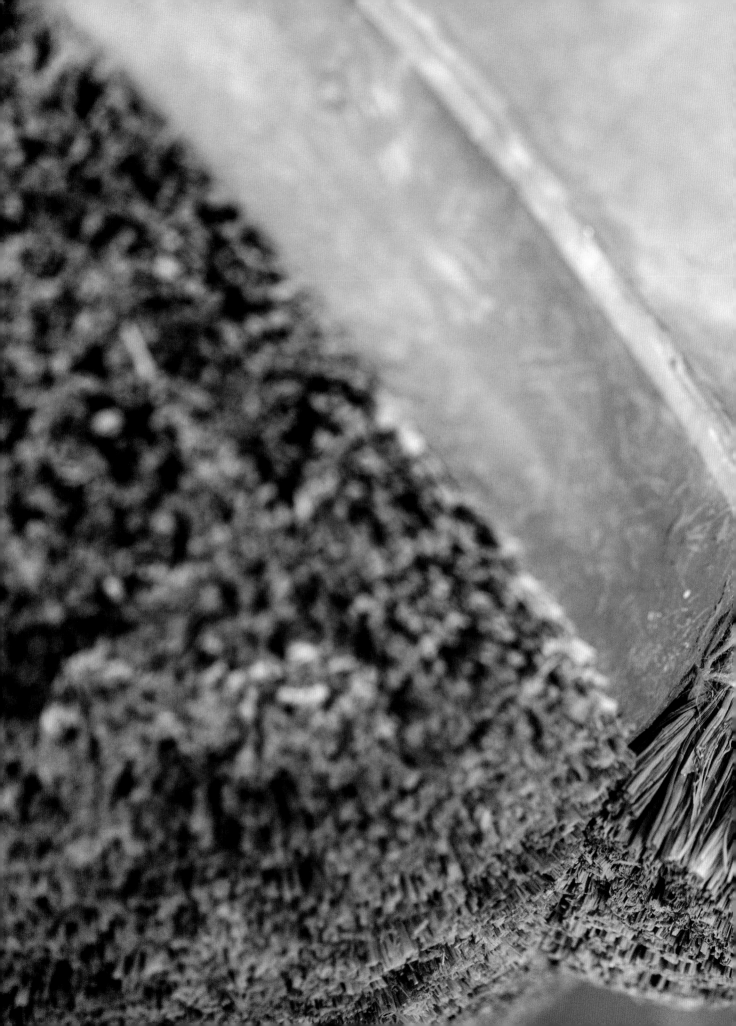

by

*Kelli Morgan*

# In July 2017, I received an intriguing email from Chad Curtis at Temple University's Tyler School of Art. He asked if I was interested in teaching a graduate seminar on Contemporary

Topics in Craft. Initially I hesitated to respond affirmatively, since I've never considered myself to be an art maker; rather, I'm a critical analyst of numerous artistic styles, movements, and histories. I didn't feel that I possessed the skills to teach a seminar on craft to MFA students in the process of developing their own artist practice. Yet, the universe had different plans for me.

OPPOSITE | BARBARA BULLOCK, *SOMETIMES IN THE STRANGEST PLACES*, 2013. ACRYLIC PAINT, HEAVY WATERCOLOR PAPER, MATTE MEDIUM. *COURTESY OF THE ARTIST AND SERAPHIN GALLERY*

It turned out that Curtis was searching for an instructor who could help students investigate the different ways that artists have explored the meaning and production of craft and fine art, through subject matter such as the history of slavery, class, various concepts of feminism, queer politics, etc. I got excited. This would be the first time that my proficiency in cultural studies would lend itself to the education of future artists. Set firmly within the geographical and sociopolitical contexts of North Philadelphia, we embarked on a semester of work that examined the implications of race, class, and gender on the lives of craft artists.

Class began like any other graduate seminar. We introduced ourselves, read over the syllabus, and discussed my plans for navigating us through the course materials, which were delineated into four themes:

1. What is Craft? What is Art? What is Contemporary? What is American?
2. Craft and Social Practice
3. Black Methodological Materialities
4. Contemporary Curatorial Praxis

... Craft has always been a means for Black women to subvert systematic oppression. In their hands, the artistic, symbolic, cultural, political, and economic converge in a single work.

The course centered on Black women's creative practices as a lens through which to complicate the ways we're taught to understand contemporary art, American identity, and the problematic hierarchy between fine art and craft. For instance, in the first section of the course we engaged Glenn Adamson's seminal text *Thinking through Craft*. Through an in-depth examination of Harriet Powers's *Bible Quilt* (1885–86), we considered craft in theoretical terms—as his introduction states, "craft as an idea."[1] We discussed what it meant for Powers, an African American woman born into slavery in Georgia, and working in the post-Reconstruction era, to first conceptualize and then craft an excellent textile, which served much more than aesthetic purposes.[2] For her and many other Black women, craft functioned as an aesthetic vehicle to self-determination and economic freedom.

In that regard, craft has always been a means for Black women to subvert systematic oppression. In their hands, the artistic, symbolic, cultural, political, and economic converge in a single work. This discussion of Powers cultivated an invigorating dialogue, as the students, who also saw their work and practices in similar ways, felt that there was no specific outlet at Tyler through which they could discuss this or the works of other artists of color more significantly.

OVERLEAF

ROBERTO LUGO TEACHING POTTERY, NORRIS SQUARE PARK, IN COLLABORATION WITH THE CLAY STUDIO

WITH FUNDING FROM THE PEW CENTER FOR ARTS & HERITAGE, 2018

The course took a sharp turn at that point, and we abandoned the structure of the classroom for the broader configuration of various arts communities around the city. We took in as many shows and arts institutions as we could, beginning with exhibitions that included Black women craft artists. We saw *A Collaborative Language: Selections from the Experimental Printmaking Institute* at the Pennsylvania Academy of the Fine Arts (PAFA), and *Gardens of the Mind: Echoes of the Feminine View* at the African American Museum in Philadelphia (AAMP). Each institution introduced the students to a myriad of Black artists whose work not only is steeped in craft but is highly regarded as quintessential examples of American contemporary art. In-gallery discussions of works by Martha Jackson Jarvis, Barbara Bullock, David Driskell, Joiri Minaya, Alison Saar, Simone Leigh, Faith Ringgold, and Maren Hassinger showed the students in real time what Powers's quilt represented historically: that they could in fact make work that was at once aesthetically beautiful, technically sound, and deeply engaged in social practice.

An important encounter for the students in both museum visits was the work of Philadelphia artist Barbara Bullock. Her highly sculpted works on paper demonstrate how craft and fine art can go hand in hand—as indeed they do for most established artists. More importantly, Bullock's work offered an entry point into African American art communities in Germantown, such as the Colored Girls Museum, Greene Street Studios, and Rush Arts Philly, which celebrate the accomplishments of Black artists across the country.

To further illustrate this point, we visited the Clay Studio with its director, Jennifer Zwilling, who was in the initial planning phases of the institution's relocation from Old City to South Kensington. Along with her explanation of the resources and opportunities available at the Clay Studio for the public and artists alike, Zwilling's eloquent but pointed explanation of the pitfalls of gentrification captivated the students. She argued that an arts organization must participate in an ongoing dialogue with the community it's entering as a result of redevelopment. Hearing her thoughts on the delicacy and difficulties of such conversations, especially in the class and racial contexts of Kensington, the students discovered that diversity in the Philadelphia craft community only begins with the exhibition of artists of color.

I think in the end, the course revealed the value in developing a nuanced way of "looking." The course didn't simply introduce them to Philadelphia's craft community; it taught them how to see the crafts already present elsewhere. ✮

*Notes*

1   Glenn Adamson, *Thinking through Craft* (Oxford: Berg, 2007).

2   For more information on Harriet Powers and her quilt making, see Lisa Farrington, *Creating Their Own Image: The History of African-American Women Artists* (Oxford: Oxford University Press, 2005), 38–42.

# PERCY STREET MURAL

Mural artist David Guinn and lighting designer
Drew Billiau collaborated to create "The Electric
Street," a mural on Percy Street, near the
so-called "cheesesteak triangle" of South Philly.
The project combines traditional painted mural
art with low-energy Flexineon LEDs. These two
properties are the first phase of the project, with
the goal of extending it throughout the full block.
The idea is to revitalize a neglected street and to
bring safety to the area by attracting foot traffic.

PHOTOGRAPHS BY JESSICA KOURKOUNIS

PHILADELPHIA-BASED MUSICIAN

KIERCETON KELLER OF R3DLTTR,

IN FRONT OF THE PERCY STREET MURAL

by

*Elizabeth Essner, Heather Gibson Moqtaderi & Jennifer Zwilling*

# Philadelphia is experiencing a renaissance of artists and curators situating contemporary craft within

historic spaces. A few of these recent projects include the *Artship Olympia* at the Independence Seaport Museum; *Jane Irish: Antipodes* at Lemon Hill, supported by Philadelphia Contemporary; *Preservation*, a shared exhibition between the Clay Studio and the Physick House; and *Graffiti & Ornament* at the Woodlands, organized by Past Present Projects.

Here, Heather Gibson Moqtaderi, director of Past Present Projects, Elizabeth Essner, curator of *Graffiti & Ornament*, and Jennifer Zwilling, curator of Artistic Programs at the Clay Studio, discuss contemporary craft interventions in historic spaces, and why these projects are integral to their curatorial processes.

**JZ:** There are threads woven through the last 300 years that help bolster our current robust craft scene, providing context for our conversation. Not to belabor the metaphor, but it seems that the tapestry woven from those threads is in fact a Möbius strip, folding back and forward on itself simultaneously. The physical artifacts of Philadelphia craft history, historic homes and their contents, now serve as literal and figurative frames for the contemporary craft flourishing today in the city, creating reflective relevance to each. Let's start with this question: Why are you passionate about creating projects that combine contemporary craft and historic spaces?

**HM:** I care about the historical fabric of our city in an age of expansion, gentrification, and development. To me, historic-house museums serve as important centers for preserving that fabric. It is an element of our city that is also multigenerational. I feel that contemporary-art installations offer these settings an opportunity to engage their own histories, in ways that prove more resonant to their audience members—both their existing members as well as new visitors. Historic-house museums can be neighborhood centers, yet they also draw audiences from beyond their immediate vicinity. With *Graffiti & Ornament*, we have generous funding from the Knight Foundation and are able to offer free programming and outreach.

LEO TECOSKY (WITH SIMON KLENELL), BLOWN, SCULPTED, ASSEMBLED, AND CUT GLASS. AS DISPLAYED IN
*GRAFFITI & ORNAMENT* AT THE HISTORIC HAMILTON MANSION AT THE WOODLANDS IN WEST PHILADELPHIA.
PHOTO: PAST PRESENT PROJECTS OF CULTURETRUST

*Crafting History: A Roundtable Conversation — Elizabeth Essner, Heather Gibson Moqtaderi, Jennifer Zwilling*

I think it's interesting that we're all contemporary craft curators, and we are talking about the utility of contemporary craft. It gets meta: How does functional art function as art? We all feel that there's a larger goal there. That's very meaningful to me.

—HEATHER GIBSON MOQTADERI

**EE:** It can be easy to think of history as static and predetermined, but our understanding of it is dynamic—our relationship to the past is always changing. Welcoming artists into that conversation reveals new perspectives. With craft in particular, our familiarity with the materials amplifies our ability to connect both to contemporary art and to art of the past. The viewer has a natural access point: you don't have to explain to anybody what a ceramic feels like in your hand. That tactile knowledge allows you to intrinsically connect your own experiences with those of the artist, or people from long ago.

**JZ:** Yes, and when something is so second nature, it's difficult to express verbally. I feel that is one of the reasons craft is such a powerful connector across eras. Something like a vessel, a universal object, can be a visceral connection with people who lived a hundred or a thousand years ago. It allows us to feel closer to the rest of our fellow humans living around the world today. It feels important at this political moment that we work to reconnect, and highlight our basic similarities, to counteract the negativity pervading the civic sphere.

**HM:** People are also reacting to our increasingly digitized world, looking for opportunities to engage with tactility and community-based interactions. House museums and contemporary craft both facilitate this kind of opportunity to explore the relationship between looking and touching.

**EE:** Everybody knows the vessel. It is an object type that is both sacred and everyday and can be a natural entry point when you are reaching out to broad audiences. This universal knowledge is an equalizer, both for those who have never been to these spaces before, and people who have traditionally celebrated them. It offers a connection for both of those groups. It's multigenerational, as Heather said.

**JZ:** That's a good point about audience integration. The population interested in history is presented with contemporary craft as part of the continuum of Philadelphia making that stretches back hundreds of years. Another value of these historical/contemporary projects is to the artists themselves, who are getting special access to research possibilities that will inform their work, both immediately and long term.

**EE:** Yes, artists are generally interested in other people's creativity. If we highlight those who are already connecting to history in their own practice, artists who are spending hours and hours in libraries and archives to enrich their practices, other artists can literally walk into the results of that research. The exhibition manifests it physically.

ROBERTO LUGO, *KICKING IN THE DOORWAY*, INSTALLATION VIEW AT 1 WEST MT. VERNON PLACE, WALTERS ART

MUSEUM, BALTIMORE, 2017. *PHOTO COURTESY OF THE WALTERS ART MUSEUM*

**HM:** I think it's interesting that we're all contemporary craft curators, and we are talking about the utility of contemporary craft. It gets meta: How does functional art function as art? We all feel that there's a larger goal there. That's very meaningful to me.

**EE:** This reminds me of Alison Britton's writing about the double presence of the vessel, as something that both is functional and is a commentary on function. Things can be utilitarian but also deep personal expressions. Which I think is such a beautiful way to say it. Not to be in opposition as binaries, but to make something more meaningful with both function and expression, as well as that certain vitality that makes it art.

**JZ:** Yes, craft art has utility and meaning, and so do historic spaces. As curators we are interested in exploring and revealing to others the utility and meaning in each. The double exposure of these concepts allows them to become greater than the sum of their parts. To quote Britton directly, an object with double presence is "giving more than was demanded of it."

**EE:** For instance, the Woodlands is more than one thing. It also has that double presence. In fact the house is a vessel itself. There is a graffiti inscription from the nineteenth century, a physical example of the human impulse to make something, to leave your mark. We think of graffiti as thoroughly modern impulse. Yet, it is tied to humanity, and it parallels craft making. At another time it might have been cleaned up, erased, but to us now, it's a valuable document of a person's physical touch and what they were thinking at the time. A mark on the vessel.

**HM:** These kinds of exhibitions also allow for research-based scholarship, common to the study of craft, to enter into the more theoretical conversation that is typically happening around contemporary art. That's a really juicy, interstitial area, where those factors can come together.

**EE:** We are also experiencing a reexamination of the canon, highlighting artists who were underrecognized until recently, often women and people of color. It's not like they haven't been practicing in some cases for sixty years. You know that all of a sudden our focus has allowed us to shine the light on them.

**HM:** The current exhibition that I organized at the Arthur Ross Gallery, *Citizen Salon*, used crowdsourcing to choose the exhibition objects. People had the chance to choose an object for inclusion and to leave comments about why they were doing so. We have real data that show many participants were interested in seeing works by women and artists from underrepresented communities.

**JZ:** Craft is another topic that is being allowed into the canon in a way that we haven't seen before. Heather's reference then to crowdsourcing connects to a recent surge in interest in craft-based art, which was formerly considered outside the mainstream. Many of the exhibitions we've been discussing reexamine the roles of women and people of color within historic spaces, while also presenting work by craft artists in those groups.

**EE:** The historic house itself also becomes a distinct voice in that conversation. It's outside the traditional norm for art viewing. It's not a white cube. The space brings its own history to any exhibition within its walls.

**JZ:** Yes! That's why I used the word "reflexive" earlier. These projects allow the traditional historic-house audience to appreciate contemporary craft that they otherwise might dismiss, and likewise bring a contemporary audience to the historic house.

**HM:** I also think that it is important to recognize the role we play as curators, in developing meaningful opportunities for expanding artistic practice and generating interest and revenue for individual working artists. Even artists with gallery representation benefit from funded historic-museum projects, in that they can stretch their creativity in new ways and make new works without the pressure for immediate sale.

**JZ:** It's exciting to me that I have a community of people who care about the same thing. Which ties back to Philadelphia, and why this place in particular is a great incubator for exhibitions combining historical and contemporary craft. Philadelphia is a particularly collegial place, with a large and still-growing number of curators focused on or interested in craft. We are forming a strong network of support; each of our projects is made more relevant and more valuable by the others. ✮

OVERLEAF

JACINTHA CLARK, INSTALLATION OF *PARLOUR PORCELAIN* AT EBENEZER MAXWELL MANSION,

PHILADELPHIA, 2018. *COURTESY OF PAST PRESENT PROJECTS; PHOTO: JAIME ALVAREZ*

*Crafting History: A Roundtable Conversation — Elizabeth Essner, Heather Gibson Moqtaderi, Jennifer Zwilling*

## EXPLORE PHILADELPHIA

Today, Philadelphia's talented population of craft artists and makers is complemented and fueled by a wealth of art and design schools, discipline-specific craft centers, independent galleries, dedicated private collectors, and significant museum holdings and exhibitions.

This directory of CraftNOW Philadelphia partner organizations can be found online at craftnowphila.org/explore/

**American Swedish Historical Museum**
1900 Pattison Avenue
Philadelphia, PA
americanswedish.org

**Art in City Hall and Office of Arts, Culture and the Creative Economy**
City Hall, Room 116
Philadelphia, PA
creativephl.org

**Bahdeebahdu**
1522 North American Street
Philadelphia, PA
bahdeebahdu.com

**Bok Building**
1901 South 9th Street
Philadelphia, PA
buildingbok.com

**The Center for Art in Wood**
141 North 3rd Street
Philadelphia, PA
centerforartinwood.org

**Center for Emerging Visual Artists**
The Barclay
237 South 18th Street, Suite 3A
Philadelphia, PA
cfeva.org

**The Clay Studio**
137 North 2nd Street
Philadelphia, PA
theclaystudio.org

**Crane Arts**
1400 North American Street
Philadelphia, PA
cranearts.com

**East Falls Glassworks**

3510 Scotts Lane

Philadelphia, PA

eastfallsglass.com


**Fabric Workshop and Museum**

1214 Arch Street

Philadelphia, PA

fabricworkshopandmuseum.org


**George Nakashima Woodworkers**

1847 Aquetong Rd

New Hope, PA

nakashimawoodworkers.com


**Globe Dye Works**

4500 Worth Street

Philadelphia, PA

globedyeworks.com


**Gravers Lane Gallery**

8405 Germantown Avenue

Philadelphia, PA

graverslanegallery.com


**Icebox Project Space**

1400 North American Street

Philadelphia, PA

iceboxprojectspace.com


**InLiquid**

1400 North American Street #314

Philadelphia, PA

inliquid.org


**Institute of Contemporary Art**

118 South 36th Street

Philadelphia, PA

icaphila.org


**The Kimmel Center for the Performing Arts**

300 South Broad Street

Philadelphia, PA

kimmelcenter.org


**MaKen Studios**

3525 I Street

Philadelphia, PA

makenstudios.com


**Moderne Gallery**

2220 East Allegheny Avenue

Philadelphia, PA

modernegallery.com

**Moore College of Art & Design and the Galleries at Moore**
1916 Race Street
Philadelphia, PA
moore.edu

**Pennsylvania Academy of the Fine Arts**
118–128 North Broad Street
Philadelphia, PA
pafa.org

**National Liberty Museum**
321 Chestnut Street
Philadelphia, PA
libertymuseum.org

**Philadelphia Art Alliance at the University of the Arts**
251 South 18th Street
Philadelphia, PA
philartalliance.org

**NextFab**
2025 Washington Avenue
and 1227 North 4th Street
Philadelphia, PA
nextfab.com

**Philadelphia Dumpster Divers**
c/o Dupree Gallery
703 South 6th Street
Philadelphia, PA
dumpsterdivers.org

**Old City District**
231 Market Street
Philadelphia, PA
oldcitydistrict.org

**Philadelphia Museum of Art**
2600 Benjamin Franklin Parkway
Philadelphia, PA
philamuseum.org

**Paradigm Gallery**
746 South 4th Street
Philadelphia, PA
paradigmarts.org

**Philadelphia Museum of Art
Contemporary Craft Show**
The Women's Committee of the
Philadelphia Museum of Art
P.O. Box 7646
Philadelphia, PA
pmacraftshow.org

**Philadelphia's Magic Gardens**
1020 South Street
Philadelphia, PA
phillymagicgardens.org

**PHL Art at the Airport**
8000 Essington Avenue
Philadelphia, PA
phl.org/Arts/Pages/AboutArt.aspx

**RAIR (Recycled Artist in Residence)**
7333 Milnor Street
Philadelphia, PA
rairphilly.org

**Tyler School of Art and Temple
Contemporary at Temple University**
2001 North 13th Street
Philadelphia, PA
tyler.temple.edu

**The University of the Arts**
320 South Broad Street
Philadelphia, PA
uarts.edu

**Wayne Art Center**
413 Maplewood Avenue
Wayne, PA
wayneart.org

**Wexler Gallery**
201 North 3rd Street
Philadelphia, PA
wexlergallery.com

**Wharton Esherick Museum**
1520 Horseshoe Trail
Malvern, PA
whartonesherickmuseum.org

**1241 Carpenter Studios
and ArtSpace**
1241 Carpenter Street
Philadelphia, PA
1241carpenter.com

## BIOS

**Glenn Adamson** is senior scholar at the Yale Center for British Art, and an editor of the *Journal of Modern Craft*. He has previously been director of the Museum of Arts and Design, New York; head of research at the V&A; and curator at the Chipstone Foundation in Milwaukee. His publications include *Fewer, Better Things: The Hidden Wisdom of Objects* (2018); *Art in the Making* (2016, coauthored with Julia Bryan Wilson); *Invention of Craft* (2013); *The Craft Reader* (2010); and *Thinking through Craft* (2007).

**Elisabeth Agro** is the Nancy M. McNeil Curator of American Modern and Contemporary Crafts and Decorative Arts at the Philadelphia Museum of Art. She is cofounder and advisor of Critical Craft Forum.

**Sarah Archer** is a Philadelphia-based craft and design critic. She is a contributing editor for the American Craft Council's new journal, *American Craft Inquiry*, and a regular contributor to *Hyperallergic*. Her articles and reviews have appeared in the *Journal of Modern Craft*, *Modern Magazine*, *Studio Potter*, the *Huffington Post*, *Slate*, the *New Yorker* online, and the *Washington Post*.

**Chad Curtis** is an artist based in Philadelphia and is an associate dean and director of Graduate Programs at the Tyler School of Art, Temple University. He has exhibited internationally, including *cont{r}act earth*, Henan Museum, Zhengzhou City, China; *The Tool at Hand*, Milwaukee Art Museum; and *Exporting Pop: A Western Fantasy*, Kuwait, United Arab Emirates.

**Anthony Elms** is Daniel and Brett Sundheim Chief Curator at the Institute of Contemporary Art (ICA) in Philadelphia. He has organized the exhibitions *Cauleen Smith: Give It or Leave It* (2018), *Endless Shout* (2016–17), and *Rodney McMillian: The Black Show* (2016), among other exhibitions and projects. He was one of three curators of the 2014 *Whitney Biennial*.

**Elizabeth Essner** is an independent curator, writer, and researcher. A recent curatorial fellow with the Center for Craft, she has curated exhibitions for institutions including the Aldrich Contemporary Art Museum, Arizona State University Art Museum, and UrbanGlass. Elizabeth has written for magazines including *Modern* and *Metalsmith* and serves as a researcher for two forthcoming craft-focused publications.

**Michelle Millar Fisher** is the Ronald C. and Anita L. Curator of Contemporary Decorative Arts at the Museum of Fine Arts, Boston. She was previously the Louis C. Madeira IV Assistant Curator of European Decorative Arts and Design at the Philadelphia Museum of Art, and a curatorial assistant at the Museum of Modern Art, New York, where she co-organized such exhibits as *Design and Violence*, and *This Is for Everyone: Design Experiments for the Common Good*.

**Jessica Kourkounis** is a Philly-based multimedia producer and photographer with a varied career. She has been a regular contributor to the likes of the *New York Times*, Getty Images, Reuters, and beyond. Most recently, she has begun photographing set stills for major motion pictures and television series.

**Don Miller** is a Philadelphia woodworker and educator. He is currently an associate professor in Craft+ Material Studies at the University of the Arts. Miller's work has been shown widely in national and international venues. He maintains a studio and workshop in Germantown.

**Jennifer-Navva Milliken** is the artistic director for the Center for Art in Wood. Formerly she served as an embedded staff member in international art museums, as an independent curator, and as the founder of a cross-disciplinary art space. Her writings examining the intersection of art, craft, and design have been in exhibition catalogs, anthologies, and publications.

**Heather Gibson Moqtaderi** started Past Present Projects in 2017 to support historic sites through innovative contemporary art exhibitions and programming. Moqtaderi is assistant director and associate curator at the University of Pennsylvania's Arthur Ross Gallery, and she has independently curated exhibitions at the Ebenezer Maxwell Mansion, Delaware Art Museum, Stockton University, and Temple University. Since 2010 Heather has served as an adjunct professor of design history at Drexel University.

**Kelli Morgan** earned her doctorate in Afro-American Studies and Graduate Certificate in Public History—Museum Studies from the University of Massachusetts Amherst. Morgan has worked in a variety of curatorial, programming, teaching, and research positions. Currently, Dr. Morgan is associate curator of American Art at the Indianapolis Museum of Art at Newfields.

**Jennifer Zwilling** joined the Clay Studio in January 2015 from the Philadelphia Museum of Art, where she was assistant curator for American Decorative Arts and Contemporary Craft. She taught History of Modern Craft at Tyler School of Art for ten years, as well as American Art History at the Pennsylvania Academy of the Fine Arts.

## ACKNOWLEDGMENTS

CraftNOW expresses its thanks to all who made this publication possible, including Leila Cartier, executive director, who oversaw the project; editor Glenn Adamson; contributors Elisabeth Agro, Sarah Archer, Chad Curtis, Anthony Elms, Elizabeth Essner, Michelle Millar Fisher, Don Miller, Jennifer-Navva Milliken, Heather Gibson Moqtaderi, Kelli Morgan, and Jennifer Zwilling; Jessica Kourkounis, whose beautiful photographs do so much to give depth and interest to the publication; Erika Brask and Dan Saal of Wonderfull Design, for their brilliant graphic design; all those who kindly provided images and reproduction rights; and our colleagues at Schiffer Publishing, Ltd.

CraftNOW Philadelphia is made possible through a collaborative partnership, with the University of the Arts serving as our fiscal agent.